The Mountain Marathon Book

By

Stuart Ferguson

and

Keven Shevels

TRAIL GUIDES
publications

First published in Great Britain in 2011 by Trailguides Limited.
www.trailguides.co.uk

ISBN 978-1-905444-49-6

Trailguides Limited
35 Carmel Road South
Darlington
Co Durham DL3 8DQ

Cover design and artwork by Steve Gustard

Contents

1. Introduction.

The Mountain Marathon has one of the fastest growing fan bases of all outdoor sports. Over recent years the number of people participating in this form of demanding outdoor challenge has grown considerably as has the number of events.

With the need to travel over high, open, mountainous terrain while navigating between predetermined points and yet at the same time carrying all the equipment and requirements for a multi-day expedition, this event touches on the sports of fell running, orienteering and ultra running and yet at the same time it can be considered to be none of these. The mountain marathon can and should be regarded as a discipline and a sport in its own right with its own particular needs and preparations.

Bridging the gap between its companion books, Mountain Marathon Preparation, Long and Ultra Distance Off-Road Running and Navigation for Off-Road Runners, this volume covers the practical aspects of competing in one of these addictive events and is relevant to all classes of participant from walker to the elite runner. The book is a full record of what you will expect to encounter during a weekend of intense activity while competing in one of these mountain navigation races.

Explored within these pages are such areas as equipment, training regimes, food and drink and quite literally how to compete in the event such as the starting procedures, how to record your passing through the checkpoints and what to do at both the end of the day and the competition. Also included are other aspects such as team working and how to recover after the event.

This book is not focussed on one particular mountain marathon but is instead generic and broad enough in scope to cover all the UK and many of the Scandinavian and European events that are currently held.

> Running and navigating your way through the wild, upland areas of this country, a challenge that is proving irresistible to many an off-road runner.

THE BASICS.

In this, the first section of the book we will look at the fundamentals of the mountain marathon. These will include what it is, how it is held, the different types of competition and classes, what is required to enter and above all what makes this event such an addictive challenge. Once you have an understanding of these matters then the rest will fall into place.

The mountain environment doesn't just present wide, open moorland to run over, at times the terrain can be quite rocky and this can give it's own problems requiring the runners to slow down the pace and take a high degree of care.

2. What is a Mountain Marathon.

Simply put, a mountain marathon is a long-distance navigation exercise held over upland and mountainous terrain. Normally held over two days it involves carrying all the equipment and supplies needed to be self-sufficient over this period.

The competitors are usually grouped in teams of two but in some events, elite and experienced runners are allowed to participate as solo competitors. The majority of participants do so as runners although a number of events do have classes specifically for walkers.

Despite the competitive element, mountain marathons are quite low key affairs with a very relaxed and friendly atmosphere. Many of the entrants use the time spent at the overnight camp to catch up with friends who are also competing and discuss the day's "happenings".

3. Who and Why.

So who does a mountain marathon and why?

The "clientele" for a mountain marathon come from all walks of life and these events attract competitors from the worlds of walking, orienteering, fell, trail and ultra running. Basically anybody who has an interest in competing outdoors and loves the freedom from being totally self sufficient within a mountainous environment has to give these events a try.

And the world of mountain marathoner is not an exclusively male domain. In most events nowadays a fifth of all competitors are woman, proving the argument that woman can be just as daft as men.

So what are the qualities needed to be a mountain marathoner. The main one is strength of character. This is needed to just keep going when things get rough and that they will. The drop out rates in these events can vary between 15 and 50% depending on weather conditions. This means that the strength and perseverance to just keep going despite being knackered, hammered by bad weather, having an irritable partner and just not being sure of where the hell you are is a distinct advantage when competing in these events.

However after saying all that, there is a certain camaraderie among mountain marathoners. Despite the competition there is a relaxed, easy going atmosphere to these events that makes you feel that you belong to a special club and which brings many competitors back again year after year.

In the next four chapters we will look at the different aspects that makes a mountain marathon such an irresistible event namely the challenges of navigating, crossing tough terrain, competing as a team and facing whatever the weather throws at you.

4. Navigation.

The mountain marathon is a navigation exercise while endurance running over rough, high-level terrain and so the ability to navigate is a crucial factor to participating in one of these events. Without the adequate navigational skills no runner should contemplate entering a mountain marathon.

The skills and techniques of navigation, the equipment required and how to train this ability is a large area of expertise in itself and so is outside the scope of this book which is aimed predominantly at the more tangible aspects of the mountain marathon. However, our sister publication "Navigation for Off-Road Runners" explores these skills and techniques from the levels of the very beginner to those suited for the more advanced competitor and both books, along with "Mountain Marathon Preparation" have been written to compliment each other as part of the Trailguides Run Off-Road three book mountain marathon series.

Traversing rough terrain with a map in hand. Two essential requirements for competing in a mountain marathon and skills that need to be practiced and honed in order to be effective.

5. Terrain.

With a mountain marathon the name says it all. These events are held in high upland areas that may be quite remote from habitation. The terrain encountered will be quite extreme with steep mountain slopes to both go up and come down. The nature of the ground will cover everything from smooth runnable surfaces to boulder fields and bog marsh and with every shade between.

The terrain covered is one of the fundamental challenges of these events and the ability to navigate and read a map in order to identify ground that can be easily run over can be fundamental to your success.

Virtually all competitors in a mountain marathon have a love for wild places. It's no good even contemplating entering one of these if you don't have a passion for the great outdoors. With the training and the event itself, you will be spending a sizable chunk of your leisure time out in the uplands areas.

At some point during the two days of the event you will end up bent double while walking up a steep endless hill, you will have wet feet from splodging across a bog, you will have quite probably fallen in a stream and your feet, legs and other muscles that you didn't know you had, will be sore and aching. There will always be a point where you think "what am I doing here" but at the end of the day, the buzz that you get from knowing that you can successfully travel over this rugged country outweighs that feeling by a long chalk.

Not only the occasional wet foot but sometimes the necessity to retrieve a shoe from the bog.

6. Teamwork

If you are competing in a solo category such as the Saunders Klets or a solo one day event like the Lake District Mountain Trial then obviously team work is not so important as, basically, you are a team of one and people do tend to work well with themselves. If you can't form a working partnership with yourself then this book isn't really going to help you !!

However the majority of classes in any Mountain Marathon are for teams of two and therefore team work becomes crucial for the successful completion of any of the event categories. This is partially due to the rules of these races that require the partners to stay in contact with each other throughout the duration of the event but it is also much more than that. It is about the blending together of two competitors so that the sum of the partnership is greater than that of the two individual runners.

Both members of the team should be able to use simple navigation techniques such as thumbing the map and checking collecting features and as you progress round the course the pair of you should confer and bounce ideas off each other. But it is when things get a bit hairy such as when the clag is down and when bad weather occurs that the value of real team work comes into play and with a partner that you are familiar and used to running with, then this can become intuitive. Let looks at a couple of examples of working together.

Example 1. Team Member 1 runs on a bearing while Team Member 2 counts the number of double paces.

Example 2. Team Member 1 counts the number of stream crossings that are passed while Team Member 2 ensures that the pair are contouring at a constant height.

As you can see this is basic teamwork where the responsibility is shared between both the team members rather than just falling onto one person. This shared responsibility reduces the pressure on any one member of the team and this collective responsibility can, very importantly, reduce the amount of navigational mistakes that you, as a team, make. Obviously any reduction in the number of mistakes made will improve the effectiveness in collecting checkpoints, however, it will also reduce the distance that you cover which in turn will also conserve your energy.

Tip - quite often the performance of a team is measured by the number of mistakes that they make while navigating round the course, working as an effective team reduces the likelihood of making these mistakes and will reduce your overall time and hence improve your position.

6.1 Choosing your partner.

Most of the time choosing your partner comes naturally, it will be somebody with who you have some form of relationship such as a running partner, a club mate, someone with who you have done other outside sports or something similar. However, this does not necessarily mean that you will make a successful team. Ideally, to make the team work the partners need to:
1. Get on socially with each other.
2. Have a similar or compatible sense of humour.
3. Be at, broadly, the same level of physical fitness.
4. Have a similar drive to succeed or competitive streak.
5. Have a similar level of experience and ability in the hills.
6. If married, have the willingness to forgive and forget afterwards !

Occasionally you may be partnering up with total strangers, which is not the most ideal arrangement, but at times this may be necessary due to the withdrawal of a partner or quite simply down to the fact that you are desperate to enter an event. In this case it is very probable that you will have been put in touch by a mutual friend, in which case don't be shy about asking this mutual friend, and others, for opinions on your prospective partner and take the time to try and meet up with this partner prior to the event.

6.2 Decision making.

To work effectively as a team then both responsibility and decision-making need to be shared. Hopefully, by careful selection the team will be comprised of two individuals with roughly equal ability and so making joint decisions should come fairly naturally and this process can be enhanced by training together as a team on a regular basis.

When making decisions both parties in the team should be able to feel that they can contribute to the final outcome. Relying on just the one partner can reduce the effectiveness of the team, the old phrase of "two heads are better than one" certainly has its origins in truth and especially with regard to mountain marathons. Both partners need to feel involved in this process in order to gain the best performance and it can be surprising how much of an effect the excluding of one partner can have even to a deterioration in the actual running abilities of the pair.

Not being included can bring simmering discontent leading to resentment and ultimately to a "well why should I care how well we do" attitude giving poor times over the course and resulting in bad feeling between the pair. The image of a mountain marathon team being a well-oiled machine second-thinking each other isn't always true and bad words between various partners has been known to happen during an event.

6.3 Communication.

You should be talking to your partner continuously but not just idle chit-chat about movies, girls, boys or whatever. Communication between the pair of you should involve confirming route choice, checking features as you pass them, confirmation that you both think that you are in the same place, deciding whether amendments need to be made to your route, what's going right, what's going wrong, how you're feeling, how your partner is feeling, is your performance deteriorating, what's the weather doing. The list can be endless but the principle is to make sure that you are both aware of what is happening to you and around the pair of you and that the mental processes of the two of you agree in what you are doing and what you are planning to do.

Tip - the pair that rarely talk to each other and don't discuss options and performance never perform as well as those that do.

Consultation and agreement, the key to a successful partnership.

6.4 Task sharing.

As with decision making, share the relevant tasks out between you, for example, while one of you is dibbing the dibber at the control, the other could be determining the direction to leave so that you follow your route choice to the next control. Sharing tasks saves time, which in turn determines your overall performance round the course. There should never be a point during the marathon where one partner is stood doing nothing while their team-mate is performing a task. Always keep moving on and pushing the activities forward, rather than standing still while your partner is doing something, look ahead to see what is coming next and what you can do to set the ball rolling.

6.5 Checking each other's actions.

Mistakes happen. With a mountain marathon it is quite often the pair who make the fewest mistakes that win the event, therefore, to improve your overall time you must try to reduce the number of mistakes to as few as possible.

One way of doing this is to use your partner to double check your actions and decisions. Two heads are better than one and a second look at a route choice, for example, may just find a slight improvement on it.

Checking each other's actions does sound like duplication with a resulting slowness and time wasting. However, regular training as a team and familiarity with each other can make this process so much like second nature that it happens without any effort at all.

6.6 Fatigue.

There is a lot of mention throughout this book about how tiring and gruelling this event can be and you can virtually guarantee that over two long days of running over open countryside then, at some point, one of you will start to suffer from fatigue. This "moment" may not last very long and usually it is quickly resolved by slowing down the pace, taking a break and/or consuming some food and drink. However, it will happen and over the course of the two days it is quite likely to happen, albeit at separate points in time, to each of you.

As well as affecting the physical functions, fatigue also has an effect on the brain functions and the probability of making mistakes in navigation and decision-making is greatly increased when in a tired condition. Unfortunately the person who is fatigued and making the mistakes is not necessarily the first person to spot this and it can quite often be the partner who has the first inkling.

Working together as an effective team can help mitigate the effects of fatigue and reduce the chances of any errors being made. Each partner should keep an eye open on each other watching for signs of tiredness and mistakes being made.

Partners should be supportive of each other, being prepared to slow the pace down or stopping to take a break when one of them is having a bad moment and not putting the partner who is suffering under any undue pressure to keep going. At the same time the "suffering" partner should be prepared to accept help and advice from his team-mate without necessarily becoming "the martyr" who has to keep going because he doesn't want to let the team down. Working together with a bit of give and take can get you through most bad spots and will, generally, ensure that the team, as a unit, will give its best.

6.7 Training as a team.

As you will gather from the rest of this chapter, with the mountain marathon there is a great emphasis on working together as an effective team and this can only be done by quite literally working and running together and through this becoming familiar with each other. If you watch two teams competing it is always easy to spot which pair have been running together as a team for a number of years compared to one that has not.

Regular training under similar conditions as a marathon, long runs with full kit and navigating as you go, will help blend the pair of you into a unit. This will give the opportunity to get to know each other, understand each other's strengths and weaknesses, decide who is doing what, understand each other's sense of humour and get to know what makes each other ratty !

In most cases partners live fairly close to each other, they may be friends, members of the same club or any other permutation, in which case regular training sessions together should not present much of a problem. However, it may happen that the two partners may live a considerable distance apart and regular sessions just may not be feasible but whenever possible, you should meet up for a long run and do some training together.

7. Weather.

With all outdoor sports the weather can have a very serious influence and as you would imagine the mountain marathon is no different and the weather can present one of the major challenges when entering any of these events. Anybody who saw the media frenzy surrounding the 2008 Original Mountain Marathon (OMM) can't have any illusions over what a serious challenge that, at times, it can present.

Obviously the time of year during which your chosen event is being held will have a bearing over the weather that you can expect. The probability is that the Saunders held in July will have a greater chance of finer weather than, say, the OMM in October or one of the other events that are held earlier in the year. However saying that, these events are held over mountainous high ground and at any time of the year then instances of bad weather can occur with little or no warning. These weather systems can also be very localised presenting rain, snow and thunderstorms over very small, confined areas while the surrounding countryside can be bathed in spectacular sunshine.

Weather conditions in the weeks leading up to the event can have a drastic effect on the running conditions during the race, for example.

1. A prolonged period of wet weather beforehand can lead to saturated ground and a high water table. This will mean that the ground will be soaked, boggier and slower underfoot. Because running over softer ground consumes more energy then the event will become more tiring than if held over drier ground. The wet conditions will normally mean that existing springs and streams will have higher water levels possibly giving problems when crossing. There may also be a number of "seasonal" water courses that come into existence which do not appear on the map and may give some navigational problems. Boggier ground may be more difficult to cross and give problems on route choice. The overnight camp site may become damper, more midge infested and, generally, more uncomfortable than during a drier period.

2. By contrast a prolonged period of dry weather beforehand can give dry ground and a low water table. Under these conditions the ground will be dryer, harder and faster underfoot. Running over dry ground will not consume as much energy as soft ground and so will not be as tiring however it can be harder on the feet through impact shock and there will be a higher probability of bruised, blistered and cut feet. Dry conditions will mean that there is the possibility that some water courses may dry up giving problems finding fluids while out on the course. In cases this may also give problems on navigation when streams shown on the map no longer exist although some cases dry stream beds can be easily

identified. Previous route choices that may have been dubious such as crossing a bog or marsh could now be an option as they may have dried up considerably.

However it is the weather conditions during the weekend of the marathon that will have the most significant effect on your performance and so it is worth tracking this during the week leading up to the event so that you know or at least have a good idea of what to expect while you are out on the hills. It can also give you an early warning of any extreme conditions that could arrive during the course of the run.

Always be prepared to alter the clothing and your own personal kit that you are planning to take with you dependent upon the expected weather conditions. Putting in a heavier or lighter fleece may just pay off. It is always worthwhile to err on the side of caution and pack a little bit extra warmer clothing into the car. If you don't need it then it can always be left in the boot, if you need it but haven't got it then you have a problem. Don't forget such things as sun screen or antihistamine or any other medication that might be appropriate.

Your intake of food and drink in the days leading up to the marathon could also be affected by the expected weather conditions. Hot dry weather should mean

With events being held in upland and mountainous terrain, sometimes the challenge is just to see where you are and where you are going. In these situations, when mist and low cloud come rolling in, your navigation has got to be on top form in order to complete the course successfully and not lose any places.

that you drink more fluids than you would normally do in the couple of days beforehand. You may also take more with you for the journey to the event and ensure that you have adequate for the trip to and the hanging around at the event start. Expected cold weather may mean that you deliberately eat more energy food to boost your carbohydrate stores.

Don't always take notice of the national weather forecast leading up to the event as this tends to be a regional/national generalisation. As far as possible try and get a local prediction for the event area as this will have a much greater degree of accuracy for what you might expect. This may mean using such services as the Lakes or Highland weather lines.

Amongst all the other pressures happening around you during the actual run, it is worthwhile keeping your eyes open and monitoring the weather conditions as you go. Changing weather can effect route choice such as high winds causing you to avoid exposed ridges and forcing you to take lower but longer routes, the need to take extra care on stream crossings or even avoid them altogether. Adverse weather conditions, with temperatures either too high or too low, can affect your ability to think clearly thus giving you navigational problems. Always be conscious of what the weather is doing and is about to do and respond as necessary. Be prepared to do things such as donning the waterproofs before the rain starts to keep both you and your next-to-the-body clothing dry and also to raise core body temperature.

With extreme weather conditions comes such issues as hypothermia and heat stroke but be aware that as a result of bad preparation and poor awareness to changing weather, both conditions can occur even when the weather is somewhat "less extreme".

The effects of the weather presents a two-fold challenge to the mountain marathoner. First there is the "survival" aspect of facing possible bad weather in open country with just your own abilities and equipment to counter it and the second is being able to navigate your way across open country when the weather conditions may obscure both features and landmarks that would otherwise help you find your way.

In high mountainous terrain, fog, low cloud and mist can all conspire to make your life difficult and prevent you from finding that control too easily. For the "true" mountain marathoner this is not off-putting but rather an additional challenge against which to test their skills and indeed it should be viewed this way. Poor visibility is a great leveller as it reduces the chances of the fit, faster runner down to those of the other runners. In these circumstances it is often the better navigator that wins.

8. Events.

In this section we will look at the nature of mountain marathons, what they are, when and where they are held and how they are structured.

8.1 What is a mountain marathon.

A basic definition of a mountain marathon was provided earlier but a more detailed description is of a long-distance endurance navigation competition where the competitors leave the start and navigate their way to a fixed point known as a checkpoint or control where their passage through this point is recorded before they then navigate their way to a second checkpoint where again their presence at that point is recorded. Over the course of the day the competitors will make their way round a number of these checkpoints with the distance between them being up to several miles. At the end of the course the competitors would navigate to the finish which would be the final checkpoint of the day.

The competitors would then camp out overnight using the equipment and supplies carried by themselves. Competitors are expected to be totally self-sufficient throughout the course of the two days of competition although water will be supplied at the overnight camp either by tap, bowser or an adjacent stream.

The second day of the competition is very similar to the first with the competitors navigating their way from the start through a series of checkpoints to the day's finish. The overall distance covered on Day 2 is normally shorter than on Day 1.

Depending upon class, more on which is explained below, the winners of the competition will be those who make their way round the course in the shortest time or who have collected the most points.

8.2 Classes.

Within each event there are a number of different competitions known as classes. These will differ from each other due to distance and severity. Further detail on classes is provided in the next section "Classes and Courses".

8.3 Types of event.

Irrespective of the different classes, the courses on mountain marathons can be basically split into two types:

1. The linear route, and
2. The score class.

The linear route is where a number of checkpoints form a route around the course. These checkpoints have to be visited in a predetermined order and so there is effectively a proscribed route around the course as marked out by these checkpoints and all checkpoints on this route have to be visited. However the competitor is free to choose their own way from checkpoint to checkpoint and this is where the navigation and route finding challenge comes into the equation. The fastest time round the course determines the winner.

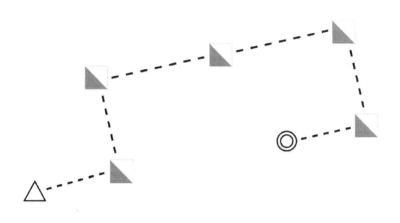

Example of a linear course where the checkpoints are followed in order.

With the score class the competitors are given a number of checkpoints to visit. Each checkpoint has its own point value with, normally, the checkpoints furthest away from the event centre carrying the greatest number of points. Each team then has a given time limit to gain as many points as possible by visiting the appropriate checkpoints. The highest points total determines the winner. Penalties in the form of point deductions are imposed for exceeding the time limit. The navigation and route finding challenge comes from determining which checkpoints will give you the greatest points total within the time available, determining which would be the optimum route round these checkpoints and then following your chosen route round the checkpoints. Not all the checkpoints need to be visited and those that are, can be visited in any particular order as determined by the competitor.

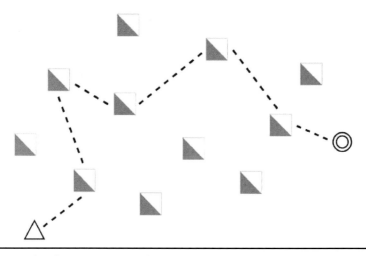

Example of a score course where there are a number of controls that can be visited in any order, each with a score value.

These are the two basic types of class, however, never underestimate the ingenuity of the course planner and in the past various events have used different combinations and variations of the more usual linear and score classes. For example, the Mourne Mountain Marathon has on some years had courses where a number of controls have been laid out from the start which were to be followed in order as per a linear course before these led onto a cluster of four or five controls that could be picked up in any order before reverting once again back to linear for the final two or three controls that were followed back to the finish. Strictly speaking these clusters weren't score controls as no points value was allocated to them but they did follow the context of the score class by having an element of "visit in any order that you want".

Checkpoints act as a fixed point on the mountain marathon course and the same checkpoint can be used on a number of courses both by a linear route class and also a score class. Further information on checkpoints can be found below.

8.4 Times of year held.
The traditional two-day mountain marathon is held through most of the year with the exception of the winter months. The first of the year generally being the Highlander held in April and then the season finishing with the OMM in October. However over the last couple of years there has been the development of shorter

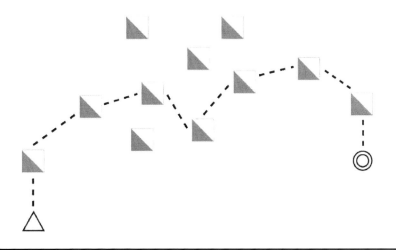

Example of a combined linear and score course where partway through the route you change from linear to score and then back again.

one-day mountain marathon style events that have been held at various points within the UK during the winter period and also a new two day event, the Grampian Mountain Challenge, held in November which is a cross between a Long O event and a mountain marathon.

8.5 List of events.

The following is a list of UK mountain marathons that at the time of writing, in 2011, were registered as being held. However it is in the nature of events that things do change and over time new events start while older and more established ones may change or even stop. So as a comprehensive list, this may be out of date before the book is even published. As general advice the writers would always recommend being members of the Fell Runners Association or alternatively the Scottish Hill Runners Association, the Welsh Fell Runners Association and Northern Ireland Mountain Runners Association. Their event calendars would contain up to date news on the majority of events. Details on each of these associations are contained within the Appendix section.

Some of the events below are more orienteering-based events rather than strict mountain marathon style. However, they do follow the same principles of a long endurance based navigation exercise over mountain or upland terrain even though they may be of a shorter duration than the classic two day event. While excellent events to compete in on their own right they also provide good training opportunities for the longer marathon.

Events

January
Warrior Winter Warmer O Trial
Held in English Lake District.
Solo one day mountain orienteering event
Website: www.waroc.org.uk

January / February
Kinder Trial
Held in English Peak District.
Solo one day fell orienteering event.
Website: www.cs.man.ac.uk/~temples/hc/

March
New Chew
Held in English Peak District.
Solo one day fell orienteering event.
Website: www.saddleworth-runners.co.uk

April
Highlander Mountain Marathon
Held in Scottish Highlands.
Classic two day mountain marathon.
Website: www.highlandermountainmarathon.org.uk

June
Lowe Alpine Mountain Marathon   also know as the LAMM
Held in the Scottish Highlands.
Classic two day mountain marathon.
Website: www.lamm.co.uk

July
Saunders Lakeland Mountain Marathon
Held in English Lake District.
Classic two day mountain marathon.
Website: www.slmm.org.uk

July
Gritstone Tryal
Held in English Peak District.
Solo one day navigation event.
Website: www.staffsmoorlands-ac.co.uk

August
Montane Phoenix Long O
This event does move around the calendar and in the past has also been held in both June and July, it is recommended to check the event website.
Held in Northumberland.
Solo two day mountain orienteering event without the need for an overnight camp.
Website: www.newcastleorienteering.org.uk/phoenix/phoenix.html

September
The Petzl Lake District Mountain Trial
Held in English Lake District.
Solo one day mountain orienteering event.
Website: www.ldmta.org.uk

September
Lowe Alpine Mourne Mountain Marathon
Held in the Mourne Mountains, Northern Ireland.
Classic two day mountain marathon.
Website: mourne2day.com

September
Rab Mountain Marathon
Held in Northern England.
Classic two day mountain marathon.
Website: darkandwhite.co.uk

October
The Original Mountain Marathon   also known as the OMM
Held in upland areas throughout the UK and in a different region each year.
The first and classic two day mountain marathon.
Website: www.theomm.com

November
Copeland Chase
Held in English Lake District.
Solo one day mountain orienteering event.
Website: www.copelandchase.org.uk

November
Grampian Mountain Challenge
Held in Scottish Highlands.
Two day cross between Long O and mountain marathon without the need to
carry overnight equipment.

November
Rab / Dark & White Mini-Mountain Marathon
Held in English Peak District.
Short single day mountain marathon style events.
Website: www.darkandwhite.co.uk

Capricorn
This event is also held on an irregular basis although the exact month has been
changeable over the last couple of years.
Held in Northern England.
Solo two day mountain orienteering event without the need for an overnight
camp.
Website: www.thecapricorn.co.uk

8.6 Events Overseas.
Although the UK may have originated the concept of mountain marathons the
"madness" of these events has spread and there are events held in other parts of
Europe and also across the globe. The general concept of these events is not that
much different from those held within the UK and so anybody familiar with
competing in UK mountain marathons should have no great difficulty in
competing in an overseas event other than the language.

At the time of publication, 2011, the following events are known to be held.
However as with the UK events above, things do change and over time new
events start and old ones may cease plus event sponsors and hence names come
and go and so this list may change.

Month	Event	Country	Website
May	Raid O'Bivwak	France	www.obivwak.net
July	Icebug 24 Mountain Marathon	Sweden	www.icebug24.com
August	R'ADYS Mountain Marathon	Switzerland	www.radys-marathon.ch
August	Björkliden Arctic Mountain Marathon	Sweden	www.bam.nu
September	OMM France	France	www.omm.com

8.7 Ranking of events.

The ranking of events in terms of difficulty is not straight forward as each event is very much of an individual character and also the venue of the actual marathon is moved every year and so terrain can differ. Issues that need to be taken into account include such as location within the UK, the type of terrain covered, time of year and also the weather. However as a generalisation, it is widely accepted among the mountain marathon fraternity that the toughest event on the calendar is the OMM and this is closely followed by the LAMM. Slightly further down the scale is the Saunders and then a couple that have been newer additions to the calendar over recent years, the more social Highlander and RAB events. However, be aware that the weather and other variables can severely alter the difficulty of any course.

8.8 Rules.

A mountain marathon has a minimum set of rules which as a generalisation is pretty standard across all events but each event is individual and so they do tend to have their own slight variations on these rules. Most of the said rules refer to compulsory kit and equipment and are there for safety reasons. A list of these rules will accompany the paperwork for the event and so it is always worth having a good look through it when it arrives.

Be aware that these rules do often change from year to year. These changes are normally minor and are as a result from the previous year's experiences and are actioned for both safety reasons and to avoid cheating. If you are a regular mountain marathon competitor and, especially if you have done a particular event for a couple of years, make sure that you do check the rules and that you are not infringing them by ignorance of any changes.

A common practice over recent years is for the rules to be amended close to the event date and after you have entered and have received all the paperwork. Keep an eye open on the event's website and also at registration for any changes that may affect you and your equipment. You have spent a lot of time and prepared well for the mountain marathon, do not get disqualified on minor details.

8.9 Required kit.

In the section above entitled "What is a mountain marathon" the description states that the competitors need to carry all equipment and supplies in order to be self-supporting over the period of the marathon. So what is required as part of this equipment and supplies ?

As part of the event information/literature you will be sent a list of equipment that you will be required to take with you either individually or as part of the team. This equipment is compulsory and you will not be allowed to start the event if you do not have it. However this list is the minimum that you have to take with you, if you want to take something in addition to this then you are allowed as long as you still comply to this minimum list. Later when you get to the event registration you will be required to hand-over a signed declaration that you have complied to the list and, depending upon the event, there may be a kit inspection.

Below is a typical kit list from a mountain marathon but be aware that each marathon is an individual event and whereas the majority of items will be standard across most of them, there may be subtle differences from event to event and some may also state a minimum specification requirement for an individual piece of equipment, for example, a three-season sleeping bag instead of a just a sleeping bag.

1. Warm trousers or leggings.
2. Shirt or thermal top.
3. Sweater or fleece top.
4. Waterproof over trousers (taped seams).
5. Waterproof jacket (taped seams).
6. Socks, gloves & hat.
7. Head torch.
8. Whistle.
9. Food for 36 hours.
10. Additional emergency rations.
11. Compass (GPS not allowed).
12. Sleeping bag.

13. Footwear with adequate grip for fell conditions.
14. Space blanket or large heavy gauge polythene bag.
15. Rucksack.
16. First-aid, a minimum of a crepe bandage and small wound dressings.
17. Pen or pencil.
18. Tent with sewn-in groundsheet.
19. Cooking stove with enough fuel at the end of day 2 to make a hot drink.

The list above is examined in more detail in the section of the book entitled "Equipment".

9. Classes and Courses.

9.1 Classes.

Each mountain marathon event itself contains a number of different competitions which are graded on distance and severity of the course and the ability level required of the competitor. This does allow runners of all abilities to compete in a mountain marathon and just as importantly, allows a beginner to progress up through the classes as both their ability and experience grows.

Generally classes are named Elite, A, B, C and D with the Elite being the most severe then class A working down to D being the least. Similarly score events are also classed with Long Score, Medium Score and Short Score. In this case the classification is based on the length of the expected time on the course.

Be aware that some mountain marathons, notably the Saunders, use names for their classifications instead of letters. However the basic concept remains the same as a grading between the different classes.

As you progress up through the classes proof may be required by the organisers that you have the relevant ability and experience to compete at this level. This is normally provided by competing at lower levels in this or similar events. Remember that mountain marathons are held in a potentially hostile environment and for health and safety the organiser will want to know that you can cope with what both the event and nature will throw at you.

The majority of classes on mountain marathons are for pairs, two runners competing as a team. However some events do allow solo competitors but this is normally at the Elite standard and the runner will have need to prove their ability by competing as part of a pair in the other Elite classes before they are allowed in the solo class.

Each individual class may have a number of prize winning categories within it such as a Ladies prize, Mixed Pair and Veteran. Each event is slightly different on this point and you would need to check the entry form for your chosen marathon.

9.2 Choosing the correct class.

With beginners to mountain marathons it is important to ensure that you enter the correct class. The accompanying table will show the ability level that is expected and required within each one of these classes. The beginner would be expected to enter Class D on a first event and then subsequently move up through the relevant classes as ability and experience improves. For an experienced mountain runner who was entering their first marathon then Class C or even possibly Class B might be appropriate. However be aware that you may have to provide some proof of your ability and experience in order to enter Class B and, at the discretion of the organisers, you may be refused or asked to drop down a class.

In the paragraph above we stated that the beginner marathoner can move up the different classes as their ability improves. However there is no enforced requirement to do so and many competitors compete in the same class year after year satisfied with the level of difficulty and competition within that particular

CLASS	2 day Distance and /or Estimate Win Time	Type of Course.	Comments
ELITE	80 km /12 hours	Run / Linear Checkpoints to follow in order.	Over 18. Very experienced mountain navigators.
A	65 km / 11 hours	Run / Linear checkpoints to follow in order	Over 18. Experienced mountain navigators
B	50 km / 10 hours	Run / Linear checkpoints to follow in order.	Over 18.
C	40 km / 9 hours	Run / Linear checkpoints to follow in order.	Over 18.
D	30 km / 8 hours	Run /Walk / Linear checkpoints to follow in order.	Over 16. Entry level event.
Long Score	Within 13 hours	Run / Collection of checkpoints.	Over 18. Very experienced mountain navigators.
Medium Score	Within 11 hours	Run / Collection of checkpoints.	Over 18.
Short Score.	Within 9 hours	Run / Walk / Collection of Checkpoints.	Over 16 Entry level event.

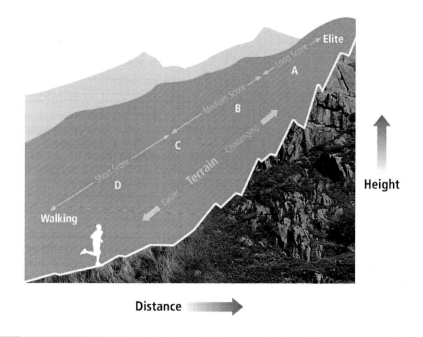

Height

Distance ➡️

Generally, the higher up the classes the longer the distance, the more climb
encountered and the more challenging the terrain.

class. After all not every competitor is of the elite standard and for the majority
of us the real challenge is competing against the course as opposed to competing
for prizes.

As a general guideline for choosing the correct class then you should work on
the principle that your expected time should be within 50% of the overall
winning time, for example, if the winning time over the two days is 10 hours
then your expected time should be within 15 hours. If you think that it would
take any longer, then you should think of dropping down a class.

To help in this decision some of the mountain marathons give the expected
winning time for each class within their entry information. If not then it can be
easily estimated by looking up previous year's results and using these as a guide.

Remember that this principle can also be used in any post-event analysis that
you and your partner do. If you took longer than the winner's time + 50% and

there is no specific reason why this happened such as a navigation error, then maybe this particular class was just too tough for you and you should move down.

9.3 Courses.

Each class within an event will have its own course and this course is made up of a number of controls that are spread around the route and are visited in order. Each of these controls is an individual point with its own identifying mark be it letters, alpha-numeric or just numbers.

Because these controls are individual they can then be included on a number of different courses. This means that the runners arriving at your control just in front of you may actually be running in a different class and on a different course to you. Their course may just be using the same control as yours.

What is termed a "crocodile" of runners following each other up a hillside. These runners may all be going the same way but they may not be on the same course. They may be just heading the same direction but to different controls. Never blindly follow anybody unless you know where they are going.

10. Entering the Marathon.

In the previous chapter "Events" brief details of all the events known at the time of publication are listed complete with the event's website address for obtaining more information. With some of the events you can, via their website, sign up to receive email newsletters and advisories on the event. Some events will also supply information updates by post but this number is dwindling as the systems for mountain marathons become more web-based.

Entering events is becoming easier and the most common method now is via the event's website, although some marathons use specialist companies such as Sportident to manage their on-line entry. A couple of the most popular marathons, the LAMM and the Saunders, only take on-line entry but there are still a couple such as the OMM that take paper entry forms as well as the on-line entry. However this may change over time and you would always be advised to enquire on the event's website first.

To enter the marathon, to either complete the paper form or enter on-line, you will need the following information at hand for both you and your partner:
1. Name and address.
2. Emergency contact phone number.
3. Age.
4. Contact email address.
5. Experience relevant to category entered.
6. Details of any medical conditions.
7. The appropriate fee.

Once your entry has been accepted, confirmation will be sent out either via email or post dependent upon the entry system.

The final details of the event will be sent to you closer to the date of the event either by post or email. Depending on the event this may be from two weeks before the event up to two days before. The entry information will tell you when you can expect these details.

11. Glossary

Included within this book are some terms that if you are new to mountain marathons may seem a bit confusing. Below is a list of terms with a full description of what these items are and how they are used.

11.1 Master map.
The official definitive map of the competition area with all controls, out of bounds areas and other amendments marked on. This is held by the organisers and not given out to the competitors. Depending upon the event and whether they use pre-marked maps or not, copies of this master map may be laid out at the start of the event from which the competitors copy information onto their own event maps. These copies are normally referred to as the master maps.

11.2 Event map.
The map that each team is issued with by the event organisers and which is taken and used by the team to navigate its way round the course.

11.3 Control description list.
A small sheet of paper giving a list of control points with grid reference, unique control point code and a short description of where the control flag is located. See example.

11.4 Controls.
Controls, also called checkpoints, are fixed points that the competitor has to navigate to. There are a number of these controls spread over the event area to make up the course and the aim is for the competitor to make their way from control to control by whichever route they consider to be the fastest and most effective. There is no set route for the competitor to follow, the route choice is dependent upon the competitor's own decisions and navigational ability.

Controls almost always include an orienteering kite and either a control punch or electronic dibber which is used to record the competitor passing through the control. Nowadays virtually all mountain marathons use electronic dibbers, more information on which is below. On some events the control is manned, on others they are not while some events have a mixture of both manned and unmanned controls.

Scafell

Day 1

All controls must be visited in the order given.
Check code numbers to avoid disqualification.

Distance   24.9 Km   Height   1530 m

Control	Code	Grid Reference	Description	Close
Start	100	293 982	Start Day 1 Track Junction	
1	144	284 998	Mine Entrance	
2	141	282 038	Sheepfold	15:00
3	107	212 053	Knoll	17:00
4	109	199 047	Sheepfold	
5	112	196 033	Pond	
6	123	192 015	Knoll	18:00
7	104	200 990	Rocky Knoll	
8	111	227 976	Crag 10m foot	
		Follow Taped route 1400m to Finish at		
9	102	234 964	Finish Day 1	

Course closes at 20:00 hours
YOU MUST BE BACK BEFORE THEN EVEN IF THIS MEANS RETIRING
Emergency Phone number 07711667077

Scafell

Day 2

All controls must be visited in the order given.
Check code numbers to avoid disqualification.

Distance   21.1 Km   Height   1035 m

Control	Code	Grid Reference	Description	Close
Start	101	234 964	Start Day 2	
		Follow Tapes 1400m to Stepping Stones		
1	111	227 976	Crag 10m foot	
2	156	223 007	Boulder South most	
3	122	247 034	Platform/ Spur	12:30
4	143	284 008	Pond dry	14:30
5	137	274 983	Stream/ Tarn Junction	
6	110	266 970	Boulder 4m North most	15:00
7	139	279 981	Mine Entrance	
8	158	297 969	Gate	
		Follow taped route 600m to road crossing		
		Then taped route 300m to finish at		
9	103	303 973	Finish Day 2 - School	

Emergency Phone number 07711667077
Course closes at 16:00 hours
YOU MUST BE BACK BEFORE THEN EVEN IF THIS MEANS RETIRING

Control description lists from the Saunders Lakeland Mountain Marathon.

Controls are not obviously visible. The aim of the event is to navigate to and find the control and while not deliberately hidden, they are placed in positions that are not easily seen, for example on the opposite side of a boulder from the obvious approach direction. When manned, the marshals at a control will give no navigational assistance to the competitor, in fact they normally stay as unobtrusive as possible in order to avoid attracting attention and inadvertently guiding the competitors in to the control. In the Saunders Lakeland Mountain Marathon for example, the control marshals spend the whole weekend out at the controls camping overnight and even their tents are green in order to blend into the landscape and be as unnoticeable as possible.

Control kite and electronic dibber next to a stream.

11.5 Dibbers.

Dibbers are now common place amongst mountain marathons replacing the manual punch type system.

These are electronic timing and scoring systems where competitors carry a small

As well as controls being deliberately sited so as not to be too obvious and easily seen as you approach them, they may also be affected by the weather, having been knocked to the ground by wind and rain. Quite often the control is not spotted until you are literally right on top of it. In these situations you need to have the self-confidence in your own navigational ability to just keep going in the expectation that the control will be there even though you can't see it. In the example above, the control is sited on a small level space at the foot of a crag. The kite is hidden by the angle of the slope and is also difficult to see as it has been knocked to the ground. It is only when you are feet away that it becomes clearly visible.

electronic peg (the dibber) and this is placed (dipped) into electronic control boxes which are located at the checkpoints. At the end of an event the dibber is interrogated and the information obtained from it used to calculate results. These are printed out and handed to the competitor so you can check your results very quickly.

The dibber itself is small plastic peg which has an electronic chip in one end with each dibber having a unique reference number. The peg is dipped into the hole in a control box in order for a competitor to register that they have visited a location or competed a task. The control box gives an audible bleep and a visual flash to confirm that the process, which takes a fraction of a second, is complete.

Both the time and control station number are stored on the dibber. Additionally the time and the dibber identity number are also stored in the control station.

Depending on the event the dibber can be attached to the competitor in a number of different ways. For mountain marathons it is normally attached to the wrist.

| Dibbing the dibber at a control. |

At the overnight camp and at the end of the event, all information can be quickly downloaded to present a set of results. The system most commonly used in mountain marathons is the SPORT IDENT. Further information can be found at www.sportident.co.uk

A dibber box at registration.

11.6 Legs.
When running in a mountain marathon the section of ground that is covered in-between the controls is often referred to as a "Leg". So, for example, going from the start to the first checkpoint would be Leg 1, going from the first checkpoint to the second checkpoint would be Leg 2, from the second to the third checkpoint Leg 3 and so on.

11.7 Out of bounds.
An out of bounds area is a part of the competition area in which competitors must not go. This may be for a number of reasons, the two main examples being for environmental reasons, in order to protect sensitive areas, and for access reasons as the organisers may not have been able to negotiate permission to use a particular area. Whatever the reason, obey the instruction and stay out of these areas. Being caught in them will normally result in disqualification from the event and may even result in being banned from future events.

Out of bounds areas are shown on the map by red cross-hatching and, if the event is not using pre-marked maps, should be copied onto your event map from the master map. Obviously on the ground there is no barriers or tape to warn you where these areas are, it is up to you to use your navigational skills and the detail on the map to avoid them.

11.8 Crossing points.

Crossing points are, as the name suggests, a point where the route crosses an obstacle. The obstacle maybe something tangible such as a road or bridge, on the other hand it may be a means to cross an area of land that the organisers have no permission to use for the event via a narrow corridor. In either case crossing points are normally compulsory and you must use these to cross the obstacle.

Quite often controls are sited to naturally lead you to the crossing point.

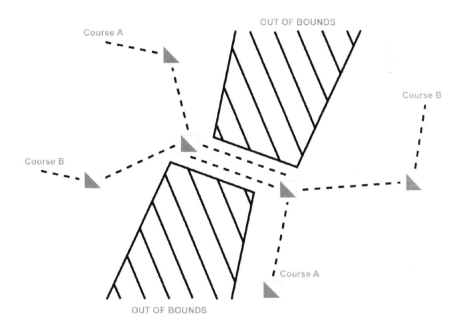

An example of a crossing point between two areas of land that are out-of-bounds, shown by the hatched marks. When they are part of the course, the use of this type of crossing point is nearly always compulsory for the competitor and in many cases, the course planner will site controls in strategic positions so that the natural route for the competitors to take will be over the crossing point.

EQUIPMENT.

In this section we will look in detail at the necessary equipment that you will need to compete in mountain marathons. This equipment will split down into four categories:

1. Clothing. This is comprised of those items you will wear while running, those items you will need to wear or carry for protection from the elements and those items required for the overnight camp.

2. Equipment. This is the hardware of the mountain marathon, the tent, the cooking equipment and the other items that are carried for both comfort and safety.

3. Personal. The small items that relate to each individual such as for personal hygiene.

4. Navigation. This is the equipment needed to navigate competently around the course. This is briefly covered here but is explained in more detail along with navigational skills and training in our sister publication "Navigation for Off-Road Runners".

The final chapter in this section covers the carrying of all this equipment and how to do it securely and safely.

Getting ready for a mountain marathon, gathering together the clothing and equipment required.

12. Clothing

As you will imagine the selection of the right clothing can have a significant impact on your level of comfort when you are out running over high and exposed ground for two full days. The wrong choice can result in discomfort and this will affect your running performance, it could cause possible injury and at its worst extreme, affect your safety. The importance of clothing can be judged by the simple fact that all mountain marathons recommend both a minimum level and standard of clothing that must be worn or carried and this is enforced through their required kit list. These kit lists are mandatory and must be complied with or you will be refused entry to the event. The importance of correct clothing becomes obvious in the event of severe weather as anybody who was competing when the storms hit the OMM in 2008 will testify.

In this section we will focus on the types of essential clothing that are required to effectively compete in a mountain marathon. However this is not an exhaustive list of what you could wear or carry while competing. There is always going to be an element of personal choice over clothing and if one competitor feels that they would be more comfortable with a dressing gown and slippers at the overnight camp and are prepared to carry them, then who can say that they shouldn't do it.

Clothing worn during a mountain marathon will be on your body for two days and so should be comfortable while at the same time capable of protecting you from the harsh weather that a mountain marathon, usually, throws at you.

Anybody expecting this section to include a list of recommended manufacturers and models are going to be disappointed. Clothing, as with other equipment, is constantly changing, manufacturers are always bringing out new models and changing the specification of current ones. For this reason we find it very difficult to make recommendations when six months down the line that piece of clothing or equipment may no longer be available or worse, may not be capable of performing to the standard that we have recommended it for. Instead we have taken the option of describing the necessary functions that are required from the clothing and left it to you to make your choice of items that meet that criteria. When buying new clothing this may mean doing some research such as looking at reviews and the websites and literature of manufacturers.

When competing in a mountain marathon everything worn or packed away in the rucksack has to be carried and as such there is the eternal debate about going "lightweight" and the question will always exist over functionality versus weight. Nowadays there are some excellent lightweight articles of clothing available but, to a degree, any reduction in weight normally comes at the cost of losing some of this functionality, for example, a lightweight fleece will never be as warm as a heavyweight fleece.

This then gives the mountain marathoner the basic questions of how light do I go and do I go for comfort or speed ? Most of this will be answered by the location of the mountain marathon, when during the year it is going to be held and what weather conditions are you likely to meet while competing.

For the beginner to this type of event it would be wiser to err on the side of comfort and be prepared to take slightly heavier weight kit. As you become more experienced and aware of your abilities and limitations you can then start to streamline and experiment with lighter weight gear.

Apart from the obvious factor of weight, one other aspect that needs to be considered is that of packed size. Everything that is carried in the rucksack takes up room, the less room that something takes then the more that can be carried. The size of an item when it is packed, or more accurately, it's volume, then becomes important in determining what gets taken and what doesn't. As a general rule of thumb, if all other factors, such as functionality, are equal then chose the clothing that has the smallest packed size.

One point that is always worth repeating is that any clothing worn during the event should be "seasoned", that is it should be worn-in. New kit should never be worn for the event, the possibility of chafing, blisters and tender spots is quite high even with familiar makes and models. Don't forget that you are out on the course for two full days. Whereas it may be possible to wear a new shirt or shorts and do a ten mile run comfortably, being out for two full days is a different ball game and puts strains and pressures on clothing that shorter runs don't.

It is also worthwhile performing some training runs with full equipment and the clothing that you would expect to wear. Shirts and tops may have been used for running for quite a while but they may perform differently with a rucksack and rucksack straps over the top of them. If there are any points that are going to lead to chafing and rubbing then they need to be sorted out at the training stage and not during the event.

The basic concept around clothing is what is known as the three layer system. This is comprised of a base layer, a mid layer and an outer layer with each layer performing a specific function towards comfort and protection. The base layer is the one that is worn next to the skin, the mid layer on top of that and finally the outer layer above the mid layer.

12.1 Base Layer.

The base layer is worn next to the skin and is relatively tight fitting. This layer performs two functions:
1. Through the thermal properties of the material it provides an element of temperature control,
2. Through the wicking properties of the material it moves sweat and moisture away from the skin ensuring that the skin stays dry and warm.

This base layer is the important foundation section of your layering system and for many runners this is effectively the running top with the mid and/or the outer layers only being added as and, if necessary, when the weather turns. To be effective, base layers should be good fitting, lightweight, durable, highly breathable with good wicking properties and have good temperature control.

There is a huge range of base layers on the market from a number of different manufacturers however the basic choice falls between either a synthetic or a wool based material. Synthetic is a good all round use material whereas wool tends to be too warm to run in except in quite cold weather. The majority of runners tend to elect synthetic tops.

There are three styles of top currently available. Short sleeve with a crew neck, long sleeve with crew neck and turtle neck with a short zip on the neck and long sleeves.

Bottoms come in both shorts and the longer leggings (long john) style. The style worn will obviously, to a degree, be weather dependent although many runners have their own preferred choice.

It is worth paying a careful eye to the required kit list for your event. In some mountain marathons elements of the base layer such as the leggings may qualify as part of the required kit whereas in others it may not and there may be a need to carry an additional piece of clothing such as tracksters.

Material
Typical options are polyester and polypropylene. Polypropylene moves moister away from the skin faster than polyester but it has to be close fitting to work properly. Polyester tends to get smelly after a while.

Rubbing.
Stitched logos, labels and rough seams can rub against the skin particularly if under a rucksack strap.

Ventilation.
A neck with a zip will allow you to ventilate the top in the case of over-heating.

Typical lightweight, close-fitting base layer made from a synthetic material with thermal properties.

12.2 Mid Layer.

The mid layer is worn on top of the base layer and it's function is to provide warmth. In it's simplest form, a mid layer can be as basic as just doubling up by wearing two base layers, one on top of the other. However normally this layer would be a heavier weight fleece material used either as a top, a bottom or both, that is worn over the base layer. The thickness and weight of this fleece can vary enormously and this would obviously affect the amount of warmth and comfort provided. The choice of which fleece to use would be dependent upon the time of year and the expected weather conditions that you would encounter.

There are a number of fleece materials and they all block wind, trap air and resist water to differing degrees. The ideal material for a mid layer will offer a medium level of warmth together with some wind and water resistance. Fully windproof materials are often not very breathable when compared to fleece and so may encourage condensation when worn beneath a waterproof outer. However those materials that have little wind resistance may need an additional windproof layer in certain weather conditions.

Pure fleece jackets are very breathable but if you go for a windproof material it loses an element of this breathability and so you need to look for other ventilation options. The standard zip front on the jacket design is the mainstay for venting any jacket however adjustable cuffs also allow airflow up the sleeves while mesh pockets will allow the air to flow round the body.

A smock design that pulls over the head is more lightweight than a jacket design but is not to everybody's liking. But whether you go for the smock or the jacket it should be comfortable and should be capable of trapping air close to the body to keep you warm while wearing a rucksack. Any zips should be capable of being used while wearing gloves.

The cut on mid layer fleeces tends to be on the short side but ideally the fleece should be long enough to cover the backside. The fit of the jacket needs to be snug, if it is too baggy then it will not feel as warm however if it is too tight then it does become difficult to wear it on top of other layers.

Sleeves should fit the full length of the arms and shouldn't ride up when climbing over stiles and other obstacles. Try and go for adjustable cuffs as these allow control of the air flow up the arms and help control condensation.

Pockets need to be able to be accessed while carrying a rucksack and should be big enough to carry something useful such as a map. Pockets that are mesh-lined save weight and they can also give extra ventilation.

With some designs drawcords may be used at the hem and also at the hood, if the top has one. They should be designed to neatly tuck away and not dangle.

There are many types of mid-layer garment available. The most commonly used is a light weight fleece. However, always bear in mind the time of year your event is going to be held and the expected weather conditions. There may be a need to use something more substantial.

As with everything there is an element of personal taste and while fleece is the most popular there are alternatives. One of the most popular is a light down vest similar in style to a gilet. These have all the advantages of down being very light, warm for it's size and they pack up very small. The elements listed above when referring to a fleece jacket also apply to any alternative materials that can be chosen.

12.3 Outer Layer.
The outer layer is your final line of defence against the elements. It needs to be waterproof, breathable, lightweight and capable of being packed down into a small size.

In terms of construction there are three main types of outer layer of which only one is suitable of use in a mountain marathon.

Type	Suitable for MM.	Comments.
Softshell	No	Heavy and is shower proof only
Windproof	No	Light, dries quickly but is shower proof only
Waterproof.	Yes	Taped seems and hood required.

The top of the outer layer comes in two basic styles.
1. The jacket type that has a conventional zip fastener at the front.
2. The smock type that pulls over the head which, because they have no front zip fastening and have fewer pockets, are generally lighter.

The choice of style is purely down to personal preference.

Required kit in all mountain marathons, it is essential to not just have a full set of waterproofs that are comfortable to run in but which are also comfortable to run in while carrying a rucksack. There is a difference between the two and this level of comfort will affect your performance.

Most runners have and use waterproof tops during inclement weather. With a mountain marathon there is also the requirement to carry waterproof bottoms as well. The same requirements that apply to jackets such as fabric, fit and ventilation also applies to bottoms.

Fabric.
Go for maximum breathability from the fabric but this has to be balanced against weight. Lightweight fabrics save bulk as well as grams. However the fabric tends to be less durable.

Ventilation.
Running generates heat and you can easily overheat while wearing a waterproof, and so ventilation becomes essential. Check for an easy-to-use front zip and also for adjustable cuffs as these allow air to flow up the sleeves when loosened. Pit zips under the arms can also allow further ventilation as can mesh pockets but they can let water in if weather conditions are bad.

Design.
A jacket should be able to work and be comfortable with both gloves and rucksack on. While wearing the jacket check that the rucksack is comfortable and that there is no bunching up under straps and also that access to zip and pockets is not blocked.

Body.
The length of the jacket body needs to be short enough not to obstruct movement but long enough not to leave anything exposed when bending over. The shape of the jacket needs to fit without being too baggy or too tight. At the same time check that there is freedom of movement.

Sleeves.
Sleeves need to fit well and not ride up with movement. Adjustable cuffs are better for ventilation than elasticated.

Hood.
The hood should move well with the head and not restrict the vision. Check that any drawcords don't cut into the face and that the hood is a close fit without being too tight. Consider a wired hood, if possible, they are very good in bad weather as the hood doesn't flap around too much causing discomfort and obscuring your vision.

Pockets.
Make sure that pockets are sizable for what you need and are also accessible when you have a rucksack on. Mesh pockets are lighter and can also aid ventilation but may allow water to enter during heavy rain.

Zips
Zips add weight and also introduce an opening which has the potential to let in water. For these reasons some people prefer a smock design which pulls on over the head rather than the jacket design.

12.4 Hat.
A hat is an essential piece of the runner's wardrobe and in most mountain marathons is part of the required kit list. Much has been written about how much heat is dissipated from your head and the importance of a hat in maintaining body warmth. The time of year of the event and pending weather forecast may help make your judgement about what to take on the event.

Options are:

1. Buff - light, easy to carry, keeps wind off but no too warm.
2. Base layer type, made from a similar material - light, easy to carry and warm.
3. Wool or fleece - medium weight, can be too hot to run in unless it is snowing.
4. Mountain cap - fully waterproof and fleece lined. Heavy weight, too hot to run in unless in arctic type weather, nice to put on at overnight camp though.
5. Balaclava - traditional woollen hat now made in a number of lightweight, modern materials; has the advantage of when rolled down provides protection to the whole head and face and when rolled up will just cover the head.

Runners often focus on hats as a means to contain body heat but one other aspect of head gear is the reverse and that is the protection from heat. Granted, it is a different form of hat with some form of peak, such as a baseball cap, but don't underestimate the amount of protection that it can give from the sun when running in hot weather. It may look a bit naff but it can even be turned so that the peak protects the back of the neck which is an area that is particularly susceptible to sunburn.

12.5 Gloves.
All mountain marathons require you to carry gloves as part of the essential kit. Gloves are a necessity to keep the extremities warm during severe and sometimes not quite so severe weather. Don't under-estimate the effect of cold

on the hands, it can be very painful and distracting.

However it is not just a case of keeping the hands warm as cold, frozen hands and fingers will make it difficult to hold a map, use a compass, dib your dibber and do many things that are necessary during the running of a mountain marathon. Mentally, cold and painful fingers will also be a distraction and make it difficult to concentrate on what you are doing, they will make you prone to making mistakes, they will make it difficult to plot your route, to identify where you are on the map and to recognise landmarks. In short, cold hands will affect your ability to navigate.

There is a huge variety of gloves available in a wide range of fabrics and thickness of fabric. These range from thin base layer type fabric to mid-weight fleece and windblocker materials. Waterproof gloves are also available and they can also be lined such as in a ski glove. As with other items of clothing it is possible to adopt a layering system with gloves by wearing a thinner base layer glove underneath a fleece or waterproof outer.

The selection of gloves will need to take in the following factors:
1. Time of year and expected weather conditions,
2. Location of event and the altitude of the landscape,
3. The warmth and performance of the glove and also its weight and bulk,
4. Do you need additional grip in the form of silicon dabs.
5. Do you need protection for the palm.
6. Personal preference.

Tip. In the majority of mountain marathons, especially the summer ones, the probability of you using your gloves is not that high. However don't use that to conclude that your gloves would be better off tucked away at the bottom of your rucksack, like your hat always keep your gloves easily accessible. In mountain terrain weather can change suddenly and to violent extremes.

12.6 Socks.
The importance of socks is very much neglected and yet they play a very important part in the wardrobe of any runner especially those running over rough, open country. Socks help cushion the feet from the impact of running. They help stop the foot from moving around in the shoe, which can cause blisters, bruised toes and black toenails and they also absorb sweat to help prevent moisture build-up which can also lead to blisters.

In essence the correct choice of sock can greatly enhance your comfort over a long distance endurance race such as a two-day mountain marathon. Getting the

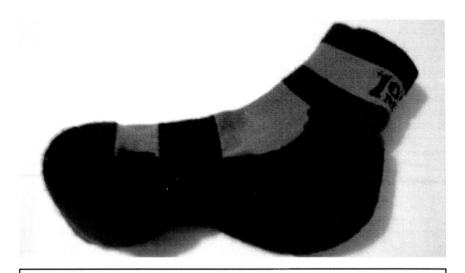

Typical specialist endurance runner's sock, padded at the pressure points to provide maximum comfort on long runs.

sock right wouldn't make you run any faster but getting it wrong can contribute to an early withdrawal from the event through blistered, bruised and cut feet.

With regard to socks, spending two days running over open, rough country will mean two things :

1. At some point during the race socks will become wet and they will stay wet for a prolonged period of time,

2. The sock will help protect your foot and lower leg from brushings with vegetation but as a result they will pick up bits of vegetation and other debris which will stick to the outside and possibly even the inside of the sock.

As with all aspects of clothing there is a large element of personal choice regarding style and what actually suits your body. We've both known runners who can get away with wearing the cheapest socks from the market and not suffer any ill effects from blisters and rubbing while at the same time known others who can only wear the expensive, seam-free, big name brands otherwise they are crippled after ten minutes. You'll know whereabouts you'll lie in that spectrum and can make the appropriate choice as to what is suitable so what we will do here is present the available options to you.

Normally socks come in two lengths, ankle or calf length. Most runners tend to go for the ankle length sock just purely out of habit and also that is what they wear while road running but it is worth considering the longer option. Because they go further up the leg, calf length socks can be warmer and they can also provide more protection to the skin when beating a path through vegetation such as bracken and heather. However the longer length does mean that there is also more material to absorb water so that they can get heavier and can take longer to dry than shorter socks.

Sock fabric comes in two main types synthetic or wool and there are advantages and disadvantages to each. As a general rule wool is warmer than synthetic which is something that to be borne in mind for events held early or at the back end of the year, however on the downside, wool can take longer to dry when wet.

Nowadays some of the specialist socks come in a number of different weights ranging from light-weight racing socks to heavier and more durable trail socks. These heavier socks have a cushioned fit and additional padding which makes them more suitable for longer distance events. With regard to a mountain marathon it is probably better to opt for the heavier version.

One further option is the waterproof sock which is manufactured in a variety of high-tech fabrics. The downside with these is that they tend to be significantly heavier than normal running socks and also don't tend to have such a snug fit. One particular problem is that if water goes above the cuff and it then flows down into the sock itself where it gets retained, if water can't get in to the sock then it also can not get out. Although most are claimed to be breathable and are adequate for walkers, many struggle to cope with the additional sweat produced by a runner. However, the retention of heat can be very useful for keeping the foot warm during severe weather such as snow and ice.

Whichever option you go for, the properties that you should be looking for in a sock are:
1. A smooth fit that causes no wrinkles in the fabric which will result in rubbing and blisters,
2. A material that can dry fairly quickly,
3. A material that is comfortable even when wet.

Obvious tip that some people do miss.
Carry a second pair of socks to ensure a dry, comfortable pair on Day 2.

12.7 Shoes
Last but not least, shoes. No ifs, buts or maybes about this, unless you have actually entered a walking class where boots are specified, then these should be

Typical fell running shoes.

specialist fell running shoes. Trail running shoes do not provide the necessary grip, they have too thick a midsole and lack support for running over the rough terrain that is encountered during a mountain marathon.

Nowadays there are a number of makes and models on the market ranging from ultra light racing models to more supportive longer distance shoes. Unless you are an elite athlete used to the minimalist concept in shoes then we would always advise one of the more supportive models to cope with the long days and rough conditions encountered over the two days.

When choosing a shoe for a mountain marathon you should look at the following qualities:

1. Durability. Obviously for the whole shoe but especially in the uppers as these will take a significant hammering from contact with vegetation such as heather

and also from being bashed against rocks and stones. If not tough enough the upper can fairly quickly disintegrate.

2. Comfort. You are going to be spending a long time in these shoes so they have to be comfortable and fit well. The last thing you need is blisters caused by a poor fit. Try different makes and models and consider different width sizes.

3. Outsole. The shoe should have a studded sole. This is essential to provide a grip on the rough terrain that will be encountered especially when contouring across slopes.

4. Midsole. Look for a cushioned midsole that is more weighted for the endurance events rather than going for a minimalistic ultra-light racing shoe but not too thick a midsole that will compromise your natural running technique over such terrain. Lighter shoes will also affect the underfoot comfort and over the two days the sole of the foot could become quite tender.

5. Biomechanics. The shoe needs to be able to perform and is suitable for running over rough country away from the trails. Trail or ultra-marathon shoes are not suitable.

6. Breathability. The shoe should be breathable and should not retain water. The type of terrain encountered during a mountain marathon is normally quite wet and if the shoe is poor at shedding this water then it will increase in weight as it gets wetter plus there is also the possibility that the moisture can affect the performance of the fabrics that comprise the upper.

7. The shoe should not be new when worn during a mountain marathon as an "unseasoned" shoe can cause problems with the feet. However it should be in the early stages of it's life cycle rather than towards the end. Ideally you should have worn the shoe extensively while running over similar terrain as your event and you are happy with the shoe's performance over this type of ground.

8. Ensure that the footbed within the shoe is in good shape and that it is doing it's two jobs of holding the foot in position and of shock absorption. Check the shoe laces for wear and tear and ensure that they are not likely to break during the course of the event.

Finally give the shoes a good clean before setting off for the marathon. Make sure that there are no bits of vegetation caught within the fabric of the shoe that could catch your foot, stones or gravel within the shoe that could cause blisters and that the studs are in good condition with none missing or damaged that could cause slips.

Tip. Many runners tape up their feet or protect with blister kits before the event, especially if they know that their feet blister in certain places. See section on Personal Equipment.

12.8 Final tip

When preparing your clothing and other kit ready for the mountain marathon it is always worthwhile checking it against the required kit list. Don't make assumptions, not all mountain marathons have the same required kit and there may be subtle differences that may catch you out plus there may also be damage that you are not aware of. And also don't leave this to the last minute just in case you do need to obtain a new piece of kit.

13. Equipment.

This chapter focuses on the more physical hardware that needs to be carried on a mountain marathon. Some of this equipment is compulsory for the team as a pair such as the tent and cooking equipment while some of this is compulsory for each individual runner such as a rucksack. The remaining kit is not compulsory but is carried just because it makes life so much easier and comfortable.

Unpacked kit at the overnight camp.

13.1 Rucksack

A required item on most kit lists the rucksack is an essential part of your event equipment as this is what you carry everything else either in or attached to. With the expanding popularity of mountain marathons there is now a growing number of manufacturers who are producing specialist mountain marathon rucksacks in a variety of colours and sizes and each with a number of different features.

It is recommended that you should use one of these specialised sacks rather than a general purpose walker's sack as they have the benefits of being designed and built to suit the needs of this type of event. They are a specialist runner's sack designed to sit in a high, stable position on the back with no movement that is going to interfere with the running pattern. However, whichever model that you do choose then you should ensure that it is lightweight, fits close to the body and is very stable when you run. In fact as you run it should feel as if it is part of your body with no movement from side to side or up and down. You shouldn't even know that it was there on your back.

As well as the basic sack itself there should be various accessories and features attached to it such as hip pockets and bottle carriers. Between the various sacks on the market there will be one that suits your style of running.

There are three main sizes of mountain marathon rucksacks with a capacity of

Front view of a fully laden rucksack.

Back view of a fully laden rucksack.

18, 25 or 30 litres. For the elite athlete the 18 litre size would be the most appropriate as they would be using the latest state of the art lightweight equipment and would be swapping and changing kit around to ensure that they were carrying the minimum kit necessary to qualify for the event. The 25 litre sack would be for the keen competitor who enters mountain marathons on a regular basis and who uses a mixture of lightweight kit and what could be classed as more comfort level equipment. By contrast, the 30 litre size would be suitable for all levels of competitor but especially the newcomer to mountain marathons and those who were wanting a sack not just specifically for mountain marathon use but for more general use as well. The 30 litre size would comfortably carry all the items required for a marathon irrespective of volume or weight.

The main difference between a specialist mountain marathon rucksack and a walker's sack is the weight and in turn this is reflected in the durability of the sack. For example, unlike a walker's sack, in order to save weight the mountain marathon sack will not be strengthened at the base and so will not sustain repeated drops to the ground in the same way as a walker's sack would. The shape of the marathon sack will also be slightly different as it is designed for running and will sit higher up the back in order to provide more stability. The accessories provided with and on the sack would be a little different as well enabling items that would be required on the run, such as water and snack bars, to be readily accessible without the need to stop and go into the sack.

As mentioned, due to the need to save weight, specialist mountain marathon rucksacks tend to lose on the durability factor and as a result care has to be taken when packing the sack especially with things such as poles. Abrasions to the material of the sack from the contents rubbing against it or it rubbing against outside factors such as the ground or rocks can be a major problem and can shorten the lifespan of the sack. If a sack is in good condition at the start of an event then it should normally be durable to see out the length of the race, however, it would always be advisable to make a full inspection of the sack prior to leaving for your next event just in case there has been damage during your previous marathon. This lack of durability does limit the use of these specialist sacks and you will find that they will normally only be used for these events as opposed to more general use.

Rucksacks can come in two basic styles, the top loader where access is via an opening in the top of the bag normally controlled by a drawcord, and the front loader where access is through a zipped opening in the front of the sack. The big advantage with top loaders is capacity, it is much easier to stuff and squash that extra bit of gear in from the top whereas this is more difficult via a front opening. Front loaders do have a single point of failure which is the zip, if that goes then basically the sack becomes useless. The more simple top opening with drawstring fastener is more robust.

13.2 Tent

Obviously an essential part of any kit list for a two day mountain marathon and one which can solicit endless debate for the committed marathoner.

The choice of tent is about balancing the benefits of weight, stability and space. The ideal tent should be lightweight, stable and secure in high winds and bad weather and yet should also provide enough internal space to comfortably hold both partners and all their equipment. A tough demand to meet.

Tents can be said to be single-skinned and double-skinned. The single-skin uses just the one layer of fabric whereas the double-skin uses two with the double-skin being formed by the inner tent and the outer flysheet. Single-skinned tents do have potential problems in bad weather, if you touch the

A variety of tents at the overnight camp.

inside of the fabric then water can come through. It is always advisable to choose the double-skinned option and that is what is discussed here.

One question normally asked is which is better inner-pitched-first or outer-pitched-first. Tents with an inner-pitched-first design tend to be lighter and more stable when erected. However outer-pitched-first tents have an advantage when being pitched in the wet. The outer can be erected first which will enable the runner to get inside, remove wet gear and then erect the inner in the dry.

Tents basically breakdown into two types:
1. Tunnel tents, and
2. Geodesic tents.

Tunnel tents
Tunnel tents are normally light, spacious and easy to erect. Their body shape makes the tent very aerodynamic and when well-pitched with their head or tail

facing into the wind they can be very secure in strong winds. However they are free standing and do rely on having solid pegging points at the front and back.

Tunnel tents are easy to put-up and the poles are easy to insert and flex into shape and, being very aerodynamic, pole breakages caused by high winds are rare. Because of their shape these tents use fewer and shorter poles than an equivalent sized geodesic tent which gives them an advantage in terms of weight. This also makes them highly efficient in the space to weight ratio making them, normally, roomier and lighter than a geodesic.

All tents suffer from condensation and this can only be reduced by using airflow to ventilate the inner. Tunnel tents usually have vents at the tail and the front to allow a flow of air down the length of the inner.

Geodesic Tents (or Domed Tents)
Geodesic tents are those designs where the tent poles cross over one another at two or more places. Due to the cross-over of these poles geodesics provide more stability than tunnel tents. However they also have a taller height profile than tunnel designs which means that they use more fabric and have both more and longer poles than an equivalent tunnel resulting in a higher overall weight for the tent.

Fabrics
The big choice comes down between nylon and polyester. Nylon can be stronger and slightly more elastic than polyester. A coating is applied to the fabric to make it waterproof but this "waterproofness" can vary. Generally the more waterproof a tent then the more expensive it is.

Inner tent
The inner tent is the sleeping space and so needs to be dry and spacious. To stay dry the inner must allow warm air to escape to the underside of the flysheet where it will normally form condensation. There must be a gap between the inner and the flysheet so that the condensation on the flysheet doesn't soak back into the inner tent. Better quality inner tents may have a water repellent finish to prevent this.

Flysheet
The outside layer of a tent. It's job is to keep the rain away from the inner tent and so has to be waterproof. A polyurethane (pu) coating is normally applied to

the fabric to achieve this although on more expensive tents a coating of silicone elastomer may be used.

Groundsheet
This is the part of the inner tent that you lie on. This should be sewn in and seam-sealed to prevent water and damp getting in from the ground.

Poles
Used to give the tent it's shape and stability. Most poles are made from alloy with shock-cords down the middle to allow them to be easily folded and opened. The better tents have colour-coded poles to show which pole goes in which part of the tent. Geodesic designs where the poles cross one another at two or more places provide the greatest stability. Glass fibre poles will snap more easily than alloy ones especially in cold weather.

Guy-lines
These are a set of cords that are erected out from the tent and pegged to the ground to help hold it stable in high winds. Some tent designs require less guy-lines than others as stability can also be controlled by the use of the poles.

Pegs
These hold the tent in place. The majority of tents use fairly lightweight basic skewer-type designs. However more durable heavier weight pegs can be purchased for different types of terrain.

Porch
This is the area that is outside the inner tent but still under the cover of the flysheet and is used for both storing wet gear and for use as a kitchen during bad weather. The door should be capable of being opened from the top to allow the steam from cooking to escape otherwise it may collect as condensation in the porch and inner tent.

13.3 Cooking equipment
A required item on mountain marathons in order to provide a hot meal and drink at the overnight campsite. There are many makes and models of cooker or stove on the market coming with a variety of different fuel sources.

The fuel that is used in the stove can be an important factor in the decision of which stove to buy. Gas stoves use a mix of propane and butane, while petrol stoves use pressurised liquid fuels including diesel and paraffin. Factors that need to be considered include:

1. How easy and safe is the fuel to carry.
2. How efficient is the fuel.
3. The cost of replacement canisters.
4. Weight and size.

A list of the advantages and disadvantages of each type of fuel is listed below.

Methylated spirits. This fuel has no need to be pressurised and so the stoves are fairly easy and safe to use. On the downside this fuel isn't always readily available and it is slow to boil water.

Petrol. Petrol has to be pressurised and converted into vapour before use and so care needs to be taken when both lighting and carrying it. As you would imagine this fuel is readily available, however, standard 4-star will very quickly block the jets of a camping stove. The stove will work best on unleaded or a refined petrol such as sold under the names Coleman fuel or White Gas.

Small lightweight cookers and combined pans are now the norm, however, because of this reduced size and capacity this sometimes means that you need to do multiple "brew-ups". Make sure that you have sufficient gas to meet your needs especially if the rules stipulates that you should have some remaining at the end of the event, for example, enough to make a hot drink.

Paraffin. Like petrol, this burns under pressure and is also readily available but it does have a strong smell that does tend to linger. On the downside an additional supply of petrol or methylated spirits is need to prime the stove before use.

Propane/butane gas. Very easy to use and widely available in a number of canister sizes which makes it, probably, the most commonly used fuel type. As the gas is consumed the pressure in the canister decreases which reduces the power of the flame. To overcome this it is always best to take new canisters to an event.

With a mountain marathon you are always going to be looking for the smallest, lightest stove that you can find. However smaller stoves can be less stable than larger models plus their size may not allow you to cook a communal meal for the two of you and you may need to cook two individual ones.

The efficiency of a stove is usually judged by the boil time, the amount of time that it takes to bring liquid to the boil. Obviously the faster it does this then the more efficient the stove both in terms of performance and also fuel economy. Be aware that the boil times for gas stoves increases as the fuel canister empties and the gas pressure drops.

The burner unit on different stoves can vary in size but as a general rule the bigger the burner then the wider the heat distribution which in turn means a quicker boil time, more efficient use of fuel and a reduced chance of developing localised hot spots that could burn your food.

The placing of the fuel canister can affect both the stability of the stove and its power. Those stoves where the fuel canister is placed to the side of the burner and where the fuel travels through a tube to the burner sit nearer to the ground and so are more stable. Stoves where the fuel canister is screwed directly under the burner are not so stable as the burner is in a more elevated position. However, they are normally more powerful as the fuel is fed more directly to the burner with no pressure being lost as the fuel travels down the tube.

The legs and pan supports on most lightweight stoves vary from around 11 cm to 19 cm in diameter. When placed on uneven ground those stoves with a wide support will provide more stability. One other aspect that needs to be considered, especially if cooking for two, is that a larger diameter pan support will give more stability to a larger pan. Larger pans on a small support may wobble and be less stable and prone to being knocked over. However, solo competitors will obviously be more suited to smaller stoves that support smaller pans.

To control the flame, when boiling or simmering, the amount of fuel that reaches the burner needs to be controlled via a flame control valve. In a design where this valve is placed near to the burner then this is usually makes it easier to control the flame. With those designs where the valve is placed away from the burner and positioned on the separate fuel tank then the delay while the fuel travels through the pipe from the valve to the burner tends to lose immediate control over the flame.

Stoves work best when protected from the elements and some form of windshield to protect the burner from draughts or breezes can be very necessary. Some stoves have windshields built into the design either as part of the pan supports, the legs or the burner. However the most effective windshield is a stand-alone barrier that surrounds the burner. This can be made from a thin piece of folded metal or else be part of the overall stove design.

Some stoves are fitted with what is called a piezo electric ignition which is similar to that fitted to domestic cookers and they do provide for an easier ignition. However, they do add both price and extra weight to the stove and so you may need to chose whether you would want one or not.

Also to be considered in your choice are fuel blocks, these are a solid block of fuel with a light frame around the block on which you stand your pan or kettle. They are a very light option which is why some people choose them but they are also very slow burners, quite messy and it is almost impossible to regulate the heat.

Pots and pans.
Nowadays most lightweight cooking stoves come with an integral pan as part of the system and this quite often forms part of the outer shell of the packed stove into which everything else fits. With these designs many of these pans are brand/model specific and are difficult to use on other models of stove. This makes the choice of pan very easy.

Tip. Don't forget the lighter or matches for lighting the stove and carry them in a waterproof container. It may also be advisable for each partner to carry some form of lighting, just in case one of you has a "dip" in a mountain stream or similar accident.

13.4 Sleeping bag.
A sleeping bag is a required item on the kit list of all mountain marathons.

Bags are made by a large range of manufacturers and come in a number of different weights and prices. The warmth of a sleeping bag is measured in a TOG or thermal rating which in turn grades them into a "season" category, for example, a two season bag would be suitable for use in spring and summer, a three season bag would be suitable for spring, summer and autumn, etc.

As a guide, sleeping bags that are generally accepted for three season use during spring, summer and autumn, are normally suitable down to a temperature of -5 degrees C. However, this is only as a rough guide as how warm you will actually feel will also depend on other factors such as your metabolic rate, body fat, food intake, exertion levels and to some environmental factors such as wind and humidity. With regard to gender, women tend to feel the cold slightly more than men so should choose a bag that is warmer.

Be aware that some event organisers stipulate a minimum rating for sleeping bags to be used during their race, for example, the organisers of the OMM specify that all competitors should carry a "3 season" bag. It is worthwhile paying careful attention to the requirements listed for sleeping bags in the event literature.

Sleeping bags may not necessarily be heavy but they can be bulky items taking up a sizeable proportion of the space in your rucksack. As far as possible try to reduce this pack size.

The construction of a bag is relatively simple with an inner material or insulation, which provides the warmth, being sandwiched between an outer layer, also known as the shell, and an inside lining. All bags use insulation to provide warmth, of which there is two types, down and synthetic. The better the insulation then the more efficient it is, meaning that you will need less of it to keep warm resulting in a lighter bag.

Synthetic insulation is not as effective as down and so more material is needed in order to give the same temperature rating and this makes synthetic bags heavier and bulkier than their down equivalents. However construction methods and the distribution of the insulation throughout the bag also affect the warm of the bag.

The inner material, which provides the warmth, comes in two different types:

1. Down. This is a natural material comprised of bird feathers from selected breeds of birds such as duck or goose. Down provides the warmest material for sleeping bags and over recent years developments in this material have made bags much lighter whilst still retaining their thermal rating. The downside with these bags is that with being a natural material they can lose their thermal qualities when damp or wet. They can also prove to be more expensive than their synthetic counterparts.

2. Synthetic. These use a man-made fibre, of which there are many, as the inner material. Although not as warm as down, synthetic bags keep their warmth when damp or wet, a factor that always needs careful consideration especially if the event is held at a normally rainy time of year. Synthetic bags are normally heavier than their down counterparts and when packed tend to take up a larger volume.

The standard fabric used for the shell and lining of the sleeping bag is nylon as it is durable, fast drying, breathable and is reasonably comfortable. The shell needs to be resistant to water in order to protect the insulation from the condensation that will form inside the tent. Pertex is often used on high performance bags as it is relatively lightweight and exceptionally breathable. There is a trend towards using waterproof materials for the shell in conjunction with fabric welding techniques so that there are no seams to leak, however, these bags may be a bit clammier than those with a more breathable shell.

The use of a breathable material such as Pertex for the outer shell will also help air flow within the bag and can help reduce dampness within the bag caused by condensation.

The construction methods used to make the bag can affect its ability to provide warmth. If the insulation is stitched-through to one or both sides of the bag, and if these lines of stitching are too close to each other, then cold spots could develop along the line of the stitching. The best method of construction consists of overlapping layers of insulation in order to reduce cold spots, this is known as shingle construction as it resembles the overlapping tiles on a roof.

The sleeping bag along with the tent are the two heaviest items within the rucksack and due consideration needs to be given to the weight of the bag without necessarily compromising performance. Obviously lower performance bags weigh less than their higher performing brothers, for example, a two season bag will be lighter than a three season one. The simple trick of sleeping with your clothes on within the bag does effectively raise the performance of it. With clothes on, a two season bag would become the equivalent of a three season bag. However, be aware that with those events such as the OMM that have now started to stipulate a required standard of bag, then it is doubtful whether this reasoning would be acceptable.

For a mountain marathon the weight of the bag and its packed size are important. However it is not quite so easy to determine the weight of the bag as the weight declared by the manufacturer can be wrong and some include the weight of the stuffsack while others don't. The construction of the bag and also its temperature rating will have an effect on the weight of the finished product. Bags with a sewn-through construction tend to be lighter while those with a

Typical "mummy" style sleeping bag tapered to follow the body shape. Note the baffle around the neck so that it can be pulled closer to prevent heat escaping.

more elaborate technique such as shingle will be heavier but warmer. The material of the shell will also affect the weight with those using more durable materials such as Pertex being heavier. All this needs to be balanced over how much you will use your bag and over what seasons of the year.

Compare the packed size of sleeping bags. For the mountain marathon you will need a bag that will pack down as small as possible so that it will take up the least amount of space in your rucksack. Unfortunately the smallest packed size comes from a bag that has the minimum insulation so you do need to take the temperature ratings into consideration when comparing packed size.

Most bags have side zips so that you can get into the bag easily and also to allow a degree of temperature control by opening and allowing cool air to enter. These zips come in two lengths, full length and half length. Half length zips make a bag lighter and also less expensive but they don't allow the same amount of temperature control that a full length zip does. At the back of the zip there should be a substantial baffle to stop draughts and cold spots developing.

The size of bags varies a great deal so always try the bag before purchase. Wearing minimal clothing get inside the bag and lie down, then proceed to roll from side to side and onto your back. A close-fitting bag is the most efficient but it is more comfortable if you have that extra space in which to move. So ask yourself the questions; is the bag restrictive, can you sit up in it, can you bend your knees and do you feel comfortable or do you feel hemmed in ?

In colder conditions the bag should have a hood that fits closely around the head. This should be capable of being pulled tight but at the same time feel comfortable without cutting into the face or blocking the vision.

A sleeping bag works by trapping warm air next to the body. An efficient bag should have a shoulder or neck baffle to help keep the air inside the bag and around the chest. This baffle needs to be comfortable and also needs to be tightened up quite easily.

Tip. If a "cold" sleeper then take one of those hand warmer heat pads with you. Slipping it inside the sleeping bag can make it nice and toasty !

13.5 Sleeping mat.
For most mountain marathons a sleeping mat is not a required item on the kit list making it optional as to whether you carry one or not. However the vast majority of competitors do use a mat of one type or another as the benefits of a good night's sleep far outweigh any downside with carrying one.

The basic theory behind the sleeping mat is that it provides a layer between your sleeping bag and the ground in order to:
1. Provide insulation between the bag and the coldness of the ground,
2. Reduce any dampness coming up from the tent floor.
3. Improve comfort by putting a padded layer between the roughness of the ground and the sleeping bag.

There are a number of options for a sleeping mat:

1.Bubble wrap. Possibly the most basic option but one that is used from time to time. Rather than carrying a long strip of bubble wrap, enough is used to just go underneath the shoulders and torso but not the legs. The advantage of bubble wrap is that it is cheap and for just the one night's camping it can actually work quite well. Although lightweight, it can be a little bulky to carry but it can be also be used as a padded layer on the inside of the rucksack to stop the contents poking into and rubbing against the back.

2. Karrimat. Originally developed by Karrimor, hence the name, this description now refers to all expanded polystyrene sleeping mats. Not hugely expensive but they do have very good thermal properties and are very effective. This option tends to be the one most favoured by mountain marathoners. Very lightweight

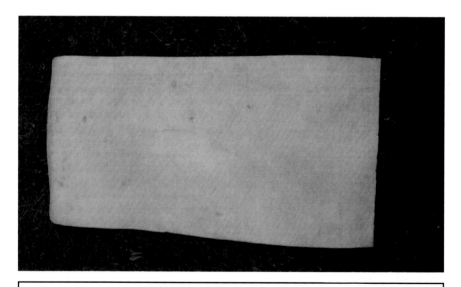

Typical expanded polystyrene karrimat which come in a range of colours. To carry they can be rolled and attached to the side of the rucksack.

but with the full-length version they can be bulky and difficult to carry. However as with the bubble wrap it is possible to cut them down so that they just fit underneath the shoulders and torso and, in the cut-down version, they can also be used as padding in the rucksack.

3. Airbeds. Not an option normally favoured by marathoners but they do provide the most comfort of all the sleeping mat choices. Airbeds are relatively expensive compared to the other two options and are quite heavy, which is the main reason why they don't carry much favour with mountain marathoners. Being self-inflated they are subject to damage and deflation unlike the karrimat.

13.6 Headtorch

Required kit for all mountain marathons although some list a torch without specifying a headtorch. Most kit lists also require spare batteries and a spare bulb for those torches using a bulb unit or multiple LED units for those torches using this technology.

A headtorch is basically a torch that is worn on the head thus leaving the hands free for other tasks. It is part of the required kit for safety reasons as, even during summer events, there is always the possibility of accidents or mishaps in navigation that can leave a competitor stranded in the dark.

The obvious uses for a headtorch are navigating in the dark and finding your way round the overnight camp but one of the most important uses which is often forgotten is as a distress signal. In the dark the flash from a headtorch can be seen over a considerable distance and, just as importantly, can help guide rescuers to you. The international distress signal using a torch is three flashes followed by a one minute gap and then repeated. Further details on emergency procedures and what to do in case of accidents is included within the Health and Safety section.

A number of different sizes of torch are available dependant upon lamp unit and battery housing.

There are three options with regard to the lamp unit:
1. Bulb,
2. Halogen bulb,
3. Light emitting diode (LED).

Normal tungsten bulbs are not very bright and also don't have a very long burn time before blowing. Halogen bulbs give the brightest output but are expensive on energy and will quickly empty a battery. Krypton and xenon bulbs are a good compromise between the two.

The latest development is Light Emitting Diode (LED) bulbs which, as they don't blow, never need replacing and because they use less power can extend the life of a battery by up to twenty times longer than other bulbs. LED bulbs are not as bright as other types of bulb and so more than one is required in order to give a bright light. Some headtorches use a high-power halogen bulb plus a set of three, five or even seven LED bulbs so that you can save battery life by using the LEDs for general use and then switch to halogen when you need extra brightness or to project a beam.

Batteries.

An essential part of the headtorch, you need to check to see what batteries are required as there are different types and sizes. Normal standard batteries are alkaline but the more expensive lithium last almost twice as long and don't lose power so quickly in cold weather. Many people use rechargeable batteries but the lifespan between charges is not as long as the lifespan of more conventional batteries.

Remember to check how easily the batteries fit. When they need to be changed it is more often than not in the dark and when you have cold and wet hands. With some torches just getting the battery compartment open is a challenge in itself and with others there is no clear indication as to which way round the batteries need to be fitted.

The batteries themselves may not just be carried on the head and there are three basic options in types of battery pack and where they are carried.

TYPE	WEIGHT on HEAD	LUMENS (indicator of brightness)	PRICE (2011 prices)
Head battery back	Up to 50g	Up to 40	Up to £35.00
Remote battery pack	Up to 75g	Up to 80	Up to £75.00
Battery back pack	Up to 100g	80 +	Around £200.00 +

Operation.

A torch needs to be easy to operate. In most cases torches are used in the same conditions in which gloves are required to be worn and so they should be capable of being operated while wearing them. Generally torches that switch between bulbs by rotating the front head or by using a rotating switch are the

Typical lightweight headtorch utilising a series of LED's for illumination.

easiest to operate. Those with sliding switches are, again, fairly easy to operate but those that use small press buttons can be quite difficult to use while wearing gloves.

Tilting head.
When running the headtorch needs to be pointed at the ground just ahead of you and therefore must have a tilting head. Most torches have tone of these but with some, the tilting mechanism can get a bit soft and the head can flop up and down as you run. Ratchets are sometimes used as part of this mechanism to control the tilt and keep it fixed. An alternative is easy-to-adjust hinge bolts which allow the tightening of a loose head.

Fit and comfort.
The headtorch may need to be worn for long periods of time and so needs a high degree of comfort. Any slight niggle can lead to hours of discomfort on the hill. Try the headtorch on without a hat and see whether the straps can be adjusted to suit your head shape and also whether the battery pack also digs into your head or not.

Stability.
Stability of the headtorch is essential when running especially if running down a slope. The torch needs to stay in place and not wobble about and fall off the head. When testing a headtorch nod and shake your head from side to side and ensure that there is no movement.

13.7 Survival bags/blankets.

A survival bag or a blanket can be classed as two different things although they are designed to perform the same basic function. In essence they are a way of conserving body heat and thus preventing or at least delaying the onset of hypothermia while you are waiting for assistance in the case of an accident or other emergency.

A survival bag is a thick, heavy-duty plastic bag. The bag is large, designed for a full-sized man to lay down inside it and for it to cover his head. The colour of the bag is normally orange to make it as visible as possible on the hillside. Instructions for use are often printed on the side either in black or white lettering. These bags work by containing the heat generated from the body within the bag creating an insulating layer of warm air between bag and body.

A survival blanket is a thin, light-weight sheet of reflective material such as metal foil or some form of foil laminate. As the name suggests these were originally available as a sheet which was wrapped around the victim. However these are now also available in the form of bags in a similar manner as the survival bag. These work by reflecting the heat generated by the body back into the body.

Both blankets and bags are highly effective at what they do and in the more general outdoor world, have saved a number of lives over the years. Imagine sitting on a mountain top among the snow of the LAMM 2006 event in Assynt in Scottish Highlands with a badly sprained ankle and you can start to see their worth.

Silver foil emergency bag.

For obvious safety reasons most mountain marathons insist on competitors carrying one or the other of these two items. However, check the rules and kit list carefully, some events specify a bag but don't allow a blanket, some allow a blanket but not a bag and some will allow either. You don't want to turn up at the event with the wrong bit of kit.

For the runner concerned with weight, the blanket is just as effective as the bag but is far lighter and also far less bulky. With those events where an option is allowed the survival blanket is the preferred choice.

Tip. At the overnight camp both the bag or the blanket can be used as an extra thermal layer either wrapped round or laid upon. And it does work.

13.8 Whistle.

Essential equipment for a mountain marathon and it should also be considered essential in everybody's kit whenever they are heading for the hills whether they are competing in a mountain marathon or not. The whistle is THE piece of equipment for summoning help and assistance when travelling on the hill. It is dependable, it is clear and its sound can carry for a considerable distance.

Whistles come in a variety of shapes and materials from small plastic ones to more heavier and durable metal cased types. A relatively cheap, lightweight, orange coloured, plastic whistle can be obtained from virtually all outdoor shops. Some rucksack designs now have a whistle attached to a zipper as the zip pull or alternatively as part of the buckle.

Remember the whistle should not be carried in the bottom of the rucksack but rather in a place that can be accessed very easily in the event of an accident or emergency.

The international distress signal using a whistle is three blows followed by a minutes silence and then repeat the three blows.

13.9 Walking poles.

Over recent years there has been an increase in the use of walking poles including by some runners in long distance mountain events on the continent. A number of UK mountain marathons include classes for walking competitors and so a limited amount of participants may be seen using them. For the runner these poles can be awkward, cumbersome and will add extra weight for little, if any, benefit and in situations such as a mass start on Day 2 could even prove hazardous to both yourself and fellow competitors. Even for a walker we would recommend that these poles not be used during a marathon.

13.10 Emergency repair kit.
It's always worth considering carrying a few bits and bobs in case there is the need to make some form of running repair to your equipment. This repair kit doesn't have to be extensive just a few things to tape or strap things together in case of breakages. A few years ago while competing in the Phoenix Mountain Orienteering event in Northumberland one of the authors had the unfortunate incident where the sole on one of his fell shoes decided to part company with the upper. He finished Day 1 with the drawstring from his waterproof bottoms wrapped around the shoe holding the two pieces together, luckily he was able to "obtain" a spare pair of shoes to complete Day 2. But these things can and do happen, rucksack straps break as do tent poles, holes appear in things as if by magic, the handle falls off your cooking pan, the possibilities could go on.

Possible inclusions:
1. A spare webbing strap - quite lightweight and useful for tying things together.
2. A small piece of gaffer tape or similar - can be used to stick things together or covering holes.
3. Possibly one or two cable ties either instead of or as well as the webbing strap.

13.11 First aid kit.
Compulsory equipment on all mountain marathons and most marathons require each individual competitor to carry one in case of emergencies. In most cases all that is required is a quite basic kit but check the required kit list on the particular event as the minimum items required may differ from marathon to marathon. Light-weight walker's first aid kits are readily available from outdoor shops and come in a number of different sizes with different levels of contents ranging from basic to more advanced. If you really want to be minimalist then it is possible to build your own kit using just the essential items required according to the kit list.

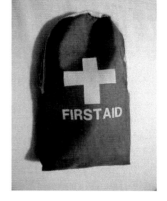

84

14. Personal equipment.

In the Equipment section we looked at all the main equipment that as a team, the two runners have to carry, almost all of which is compulsory under the rules of mountain marathons. In addition to this each individual runner will also be carrying their own personal kit comprising items that they themselves will be using over the weekend. None of this kit is compulsory and it is up to the individual runner whether they decide to take it or not although some items such as plate and cutlery would, almost, definitely be taken. This list covers the basics but is not exhaustive and individuals will make their own choice as to what they consider essential and will add to it as they please.

Cutlery - knife, fork and spoon.
Obviously used for preparing and eating your meals. Be as minimalistic as you possibly can in terms of weight. A good alternative to carrying both a fork and spoon is a spork, a combined fork and spoon.

Plate and bowl.
For eating from at the overnight camp. Again be as minimalistic as possible in terms of weight. Consider whether you actually need both, a decision which may depend upon your menu choice.

Mug.
Lightweight plastic mug for your overnight drinks. Depending upon how minimalistic you are going during the course of the run, it can also be used to drink from streams while running round the course.

Swiss army knife.
For those unexpected moments when you may have to make some running repairs to equipment.

Midge repellent and midge net hat.
Work on the basis that the overnight camp is going to be midge infested, quite often you wouldn't be far wrong. Repellent and one of these lightweight mesh hats can just make life that little bit more bearable.

Soap, towel, toothbrush and toothpaste.
This totally depends upon your own level of personal hygiene and whether you can stand being dirty for the two days while you are out on the marathon. If you can, then it obviously saves weight by not carrying these. For those that take them then obviously think of the weight factor, don't take a new bar of soap take

a smaller partially-used bar or even alternatively soap flakes (thin shavings of soap), take an almost empty tube of toothpaste, take a small camping towel. People have even been known to saw off most of the handle from their toothbrush in order to save a couple of grams.

Toilet paper.
You can guarantee that there wouldn't be enough provided in the toilet facilities at the overnight camp. So unless you have a particular fondness for using dock leafs it is always worthwhile carrying a small supply of your own paper in a small plastic bag.

Water tablets.
For chemical purification of water at the overnight camp.

Pen or pencil.
A red pen will be carried anyway as part of your navigational equipment but it is always useful to carry either a pen or pencil for such things as writing down your overnight position, day 2 start time, other notes etc.

Sunglasses and sunscreen.
Dependent upon the expected weather it may be advisable to carry some protection against the effects of strong sunlight. In the higher mountain environment it is very easy to get sunburn without noticing.

Small board game.
Dependent upon the time of the year the event is held and how soon darkness drops, you may be spending some time shut up in your tent. A small board game can help pass this time in an amusing manner.

Ear plugs.
At the overnight camp you want a good night's sleep and there is no guarantee that your partner or the people in the tents alongside you wouldn't be snorers or just noisy, inconsiderate people. Ear plugs can make the difference.

Tin foil - wind break for stove.
If you are not using a stove that has an integral windshield as part of the design then it may be worthwhile taking a small square of tin foil to be used to form a windbreak around the burner of your stove. In windy conditions this little act can significantly improve the performance of the stove.

Freezer bags for dry feet.

During the course of the day both your feet and your running shoes are going to get rather wet and muddy. The feet will dry but every time that you put your shoes back on again they will get wet once more. As obviously you wouldn't be carrying a second pair to wear while wandering round the overnight campsite, a couple of freezer bags can be placed inside the wet shoes in order to keep your feet dry while wearing them.

Stuff sacs.

To keep individual items dry within your rucksack. Lightweight water-tight plastic sacs are commercially available or as an alternative self-sealing plastic bags can be used.

Rucksack liner.

To keep the elements out of your rucksack, this is a waterproof bag that goes inside the sack and into which everything else is packed. These are commercially available but a lightweight option is a bin bag which can be folded over at the top. The bin bag may not be 100% waterproof but if the items inside are in stuff sacs then it can be very effective.

Blister kit.

Used by many runners both to prevent and to heal blisters. Most makes have a "second skin" to cover potential areas of rubbing and stop blisters forming. Experience and training will tell you whether you are prone to blisters and will benefit from their use. Many runners also tape up their feet to prevent blisters forming, in this case you may want to carry some spare tape for Day 2.

15. Navigation Equipment.

The equipment listed below is the specialist navigation equipment needed to compete in a mountain marathon. None of this is listed in the general "Equipment" section included earlier in this book and needs to be carried in addition to that. Most of this equipment is compulsory although one or two items are discretionary and could help your performance provided that you are competent in their use.

As mentioned earlier the "Black Arts" of navigation are outside the scope of this book and for a more in-depth look at navigation equipment and techniques then you are advised to see our sister book 'Navigation for Off Road Runners'.

15.1 Map.
Basically a diagram of the countryside over which you are going to be running. Maps are, obviously, compulsory equipment on all mountain marathons and are normally provided although some provide one per team and some one per partner. In the case of one per team additional maps may sometimes be available to purchase.

The map, the fundamental part of any navigation equipment. The map is normally prepared specifically for each event and provided to the competitors.

The maps supplied may be paper-based or they may be on a waterproof material. This is totally dependent upon the event. In either case it may be useful to carry some form of map bag to help protect it.

The map itself may be pre-marked with all the checkpoints, out-of-bounds areas, etc printed on it or it may just be the basic map and you will be required to mark these on yourself. Again this will be dependent upon event. Even if the map is pre-marked then there may still be a need to mark it up yourself with last minute amendments.

15.2 Compass.

The device used to do the actual navigation. Compulsory equipment on all mountain marathons. It is recommended that each team member should carry their own individual compass. In some cases this is compulsory while in other marathons one between a pair is all that is required. However by carrying your own it does mean that you have a spare in case of unforeseen accidents, compasses are fragile and easily broken.

On a more personal level, when competing we have both been known to individually carry two compasses as a safeguard thus giving possibly four compasses within the pair.

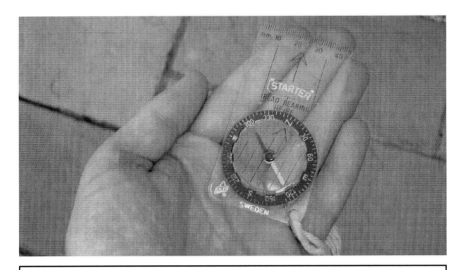

Basic hand held compass.

Tip. When packing your compass for the event make sure that it is working and packed safely and securely. It is no good reaching for it thirty minutes into the event to find that it is not there or is broken.

15.3 Watch.

Used to time your progress. If you can estimate how long a section should take to run and you know how long you have actually been running then you can have an idea of your position along that section. Not required equipment on a mountain marathon although most runners do wear one out of habit if nothing else.

15.4 Pen.

Used to mark-up the maps with checkpoint positions, out-of-bounds areas and amendments to the map. Normally red pens are used so that the ink will stand out from the background colours of the map. Sometimes stipulated as part of the compulsory equipment especially if pre-marked maps aren't being used on the event although even if the event maps are pre-marked, it is always useful to have a pen to make any last minute changes to the map. Always useful to carry a spare among the team just in case of loss or accidents.

Tip. Use different coloured pens for Day 1 and Day 2. This makes it easier to differentiate between the different day's controls and avoid mistakes.

15.5 Altimeter.

A "nice to have" piece of equipment that tells you at what height you are above sea level. Nowadays a large number of watches that are built for the outdoor sportsman have an altimeter built in. Very handy for identifying that control standing on a contour line or on a spot height. Not normally listed as part of the compulsory equipment, however, take care reading the event's equipment list as some marathons have banned their use.

15.6 GPS

These pieces of equipment are generally banned from mountain marathons and as these events are tests of navigational ability this is rightfully so.

16. Packing Your Rucksack.

We've now described the equipment that you are required and would want to take with you. These now have to be carried in your rucksack but they have to be carried in such a way that they are safe, secure, practical and cause the least inconvenience to you while you are running.

16.1 Sharing the load.

The equipment carried by the pair of runners during a competition can be split into Personal items and Shared equipment.

1. Personal items are as the name suggests the personal clothing and kit that is chosen and worn or used by each individual runner such as base layers, waterproofs, toothbrush etc. It is each runners own responsibility to carry these items. The weight and bulk of these items are chosen by the individual runner and so it is unfair to expect your partner to carry your share.

2. Shared equipment is that equipment that has to be carried by the team as a whole and so the responsibility for carrying this has also got to be shared between the two runners. Out of all the clothing/kit carried, the three high weight/volume articles carried by the team as a whole are the tent, cooking equipment including food and the sleeping bag. The sleeping bag is personal equipment and each runner will carry their own, however, the tent and the cooking equipment will be split between the two team members.

Prior to the event, time needs to be taken to identify all the shared equipment that is to be carried and then split the load determining who is taking what. The easiest way to do this is to simply weigh the kit and then split it 50/50. However the following factors may also need to be taken into account.

1. Body size and strength. With partners of roughly equal body size and strength then there is no real problem with an equal split of the load, however, when one partner is larger and stronger than the other then in order to optimise the performance of the team as a whole then the larger partner may have to carry more than an equal share of the load. This may be of particular relevance for mixed pairs.

2. Tent weight. On the second day the tent may be heavier due to wet or damp and depending on overnight weather conditions this extra weight may be considerable.

3. Cooking equipment. By the start of the second day the weight of the cooking

equipment will have been reduced due to food having been consumed and fuel being used.

Always bear in mind that during a mountain marathon it is performance of the team as a whole that counts and not that of the individual. This means that you have to be flexible in your approach to a number of different areas and this includes load sharing. It is mentioned above that at times there may be a need to share the weight unequally but there may also be times when, for example, before the start of Day 2, the load sharing may have to be re-evaluated for the second day.

Also, with the mountain marathon being such a long endurance event there will be times when one partner is struggling more than the other due to fatigue, lack of fitness etc. In these circumstances you may have to be prepared to carry more than your agreed load in order to help your partner over this bad spell until they have recovered sufficiently to reclaim their share. You never know when this favour may need to be returned.

16.2 Protecting the contents of your rucksack.

With such a quantity of equipment, care needs to be taken when packing these items into the rucksack ready for the event. Think about what you are doing and why, do not just pile your kit into the sack, take time and think about it and be logical. This and the next section will give you some thoughts on the best way to protect your kit, your rucksack and you.

Make sure that everything is securely packed in the rucksack and that there is nothing protruding no matter how little, these may dig into your back and shoulders and make the sack uncomfortable to wear. Even if ok when first slung over the shoulders, after two hours a small lump may feel like a boulder in the small of the back. Also any piece of kit or equipment that protrudes, especially from the bottom of the sack, is liable to damage when the sack is placed on the ground. When packed always run your hand along the outside of the rucksack to ensure that there are no bulges.

Take care where you place things within the rucksack. Use softer, more cushioned items to protect more fragile ones. These can also provide a cushion between harder bits of kit and the skin of the rucksack. Rubbing from hard items, in particular metal objects, can lead to heavy wear and tear on the fabric of the rucksack itself. In the longer term this can reduce the useful life of the sack but in the sorter, more immediate term, this could cause a snap or tear in the sack while actually still on the event potentially causing a number of different problems.

Thoughtless packing can cause noise and movement both from and within the rucksack. Any loose object that is banging and clattering away either in or on your sack can get pretty annoying after going continuously for a couple of hours irrespective of how loud a noise it actually does make.

Your rucksack should be packed tight with no movement of the objects inside. There is nothing worse than running with a rucksack swaying from side to side on your back and it can be potentially dangerous for both you and your partner. A moving rucksack has a destabilising effect and in the worst case can seriously unbalance your centre of gravity as you run. This can make you more susceptible to falls and stumbles and this is particularly so when running steeply downhill where good balance is essential to keeping you upright. Most rucksacks nowadays incorporate some form of compression straps to keep the load stable .... make sure that you use them.

On a mountain marathon the kit within the rucksack always stands a reasonable chance of getting wet. This can be through either the weather conditions, stream crossings and even just condensation/sweat being generated from running and very probably all three at the same time. A waterproof liner to the sack, even something as simple as a bin bag, will help ensure that your extra clothes and sleeping bag are kept dry. An extra precaution would be to ensure that each item is in its own individual plastic bag before they went into the liner.

16.3 Packing order.

Although packing order may not be high on everybody's order of importance, packing in a correct order can make life so much easier especially when having to unpack the rucksack at the overnight camp during inclement weather.

There are three guiding principles for packing the rucksack:
1. What items do you need to have immediately to hand while running on the event.
2. What items do you need first at the overnight camp.
3. Bulkier and heavier items should be at the bottom of the sack and closer to the back in order to ensure stability.

So starting at the bottom of the main compartment of the sack how would we pack it ?

The sleeping bag would not be needed until the overnight camp and even then it wouldn't be needed until after the tent is set up. So the sleeping bag would go on the bottom of the sack. This would also put something relatively soft at the bottom that would not be damaged by placing the sack heavily on the ground.

The next heavy/bulky item would be the cooking equipment and overnight food. Again this would not be needed until the overnight camp and the tent was set-up. The softness of the sleeping bag below and the next layer above would help protect the stove etc from damage and would also help stop any rubbing against the fabric of the rucksack and more importantly against your back.

The next in would be your spare and overnight clothing. Although not particularly heavy or bulky they would, again, not be needed until after the tent was pitched. At the end of Day 1 it is always pleasant to change out of wet clothing and get into something dry and warm as soon as possible, however, in bad weather the priority would be to get the tent up so that you had somewhere to change without the cloths that you are changing into becoming wet and cold.

The softness of the clothing would also provide a layer between the metal of the cooking equipment and the tent which comes next.

On top of these would be the tent. This would be the first item out at the overnight camp as the priority would be to set-up a dry shelter where you can change, replenish your energy and fluid levels and recover. Dependant upon the make and model of your rucksack there may be an external sleeve to hold the tent poles.

The final layer in the rucksack would be those items that you would need to have immediately at hand during the course of the event. Those items such as waterproof outers, hat and gloves. One added advantage of having the waterproofs at the top of the sack is that it gives a fairly waterproof top above the other contents within the sack. Even when using a waterproof liner the weak spot will always be the top of the sack where access is gained.

Food, energy bars and fluid used while actually running should always be readily available without necessarily having to stop and go into your rucksack. Most modern sacks, especially those specifically designed for mountain marathons, have a varying number of pockets and/or mesh sections on the outside of the main compartment that can hold these items.

Larger items such as a karrimat can be tightly rolled and strapped to the outside of the sack. Make sure that you do it in such a way so that it doesn't hinder your running movement. If you are using a cut-down karrimat then it may go inside the sack as padding against the back.

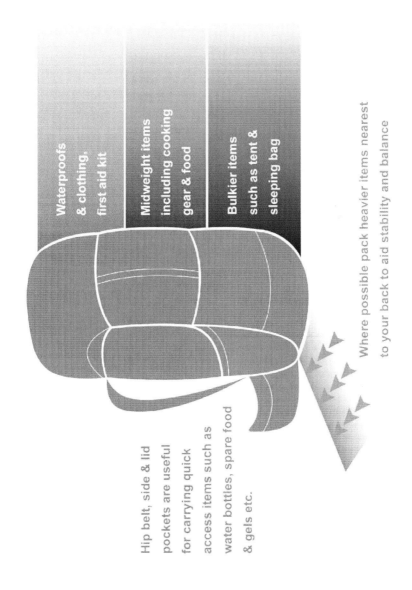

Waterproofs & clothing, first aid kit

Midweight items including cooking gear & food

Bulkier items such as tent & sleeping bag

Where possible pack heavier items nearest to your back to aid stability and balance

Hip belt, side & lid pockets are useful for carrying quick access items such as water bottles, spare food & gels etc.

FOOD AND DRINK.

The body is an engine and all engines need fuel and this is provided by the food and drink that you carry with you. Taking both the right type and the correct volume can be critical to successfully completing this event. This section looks at the food and drink necessary for the weekend, what the options are and how much is needed. This will cover the essentials and also those little luxuries that will make the weekend just that little bit more pleasant.

Dehydrated overnight meal, snacks to eat on the run and energy drink. That plus water provide the basic essentials for fuel and fluid needs over the course of the event.

17. Food and Calorie Intake.

This section discusses the food and calorie intake required to perform during a mountain marathon. However, bear in mind that what is normal and accepted practice to eat over one of these weekends may not suit everybody. We all have our own particular tastes and food preferences covering vegetarianism, to allergies and intolerances, to religious requirements and, therefore, whatever you carry to eat has to be suitable for you.

The food regime suggested here is the normal accepted practice of the majority of mountain marathoners but feel free to change it to your own needs. At the end of the day, you as the competitor can take and eat whatever you wish, after all it is you that is going to carry and prepare it.

One point that does need to be mentioned about food is never use a particular type of food for the first time on a mountain marathon. Always check-out prior to the event whether you can actually "stomach" new food or drink. Upset stomachs, and worse, have spoilt the mountain marathons of many teams. Use your chosen brand/type of food regularly during training and get used to it.

17.1 Selecting your menu.

As mentioned above in the introduction to this section, the type and quantity of food that you take with you to the mountain marathon is down to you and your own personal choice. However there are certain factors that do need to be borne in mind that may influence your decision.

The overriding theme of carrying anything during a mountain marathon is to make it as lightweight as possible. To that end most people use dehydrated food of one kind or another. It is relatively light and not easily damaged in your pack.

There are many types of dehydrated food on the market ranging from the more standard fare such as instant mashed potato and soya-based meals from the supermarket shelves to the more specialist expedition ready meals available from outdoor shops. These meals can cover both your evening meal at the end of Day 1 and also breakfast on Day 2.

Whatever your choice go for something that is easy to prepare, something that is not complicated with too many operations. The more complex a meal then the more fuel will be required to cook it and the greater the number of plates and pans required to both to cook it in and to eat it off, all of which have to be taken with you.

Most people take something along the lines of a boil-in-the-bag meal or a dehydrated ready meal where boiling water just needs to be added. More often than not these can also be eaten from the bag or container so that saves on the weight of taking crockery as well.

One other factor that most people forget about is the washing up particularly if you have a number of courses and a limited number of pans. If you don't mind having custard tinged with the flavour of dried soya mince then you have no problem but for other people then this may mean washing out the single pan between courses. This is another advantage of the boil-in-the-bag or add-boiling-water-to-the-bag type meals - very little washing up.

17.2 Pre-event.
Prior to the mountain marathon you should look at altering the balance of your diet in order to maximise your energy levels for the event.

In simple terms the body stores a product called glycogen which is the substance that produces the energy to power movement and this is produced from carbohydrate. However the body itself can only store enough of this glycogen to power approximately ninety minutes of exercise. After this, additional fuel needs to be taken on to avoid running short of energy. Energy bars, drinks and gels are good for topping up the glycogen levels while you are actually running the marathon but, similar to a road marathon, if you can carbo-load before the event then that ensures that you are standing on the start line with the maximum amount of energy available.

The most common approach to carbo-loading nowadays is to quite simply increase the proportion of carbohydrates within your diet for the week before the event but to be careful not to increase the total calories consumed.

In a normal diet a person would need around 5 to 7 grams of carbohydrate per kilo of bodyweight which would equate to about 60% of your daily calorie intake being carbohydrate. Typically this would be around 1,500 kcal of carbohydrate per day for most women and 1,800 kcal for men.

During a carbo-loading phase the intention should be to increase the carbohydrate intake up to between 8 and 10 grams per kilo of bodyweight. For a runner weighing around 70 kilos then that would be between 560 and 700 grams of carbohydrate per day and as each gram is the equivalent of four calories this would be around 2,800 kcal of carbohydrate being consumed per day.

To reach this target of carbohydrate consumption, try to eat little and often rather than just increasing the size of your normal meals. Eating five or six smaller meals is easier than stuffing yourself full on a couple of quite large ones.

You wouldn't feel quite so queasy and lethargic. As mentioned above make sure that you don't increase your daily calorie intake, instead it is just about changing the relevant proportions of what you already eat.

While your body is storing this glycogen it is also storing water, around 3 grams for every gram of glycogen. So during carbo-loading it is quite likely that you will put on extra weight due to this water retention but don't worry too much about this as it will be quickly lost over the course of the mountain marathon weekend.

17.3 During the first day of the event.

Bear in mind that Day 1 of a mountain marathon can be a very long day and will consist of running and walking over quite severe terrain including considerable ascents and descents. All of this requires the expenditure of large amounts of energy and so the maintaining and replenishing of energy stores over the course of the day becomes a very high priority.

From the more scientific point of view the exercise of running over level ground equates to, roughly, 100 calories consumed per mile. The exertion of running over rough terrain increases this consumption figure and the tougher the terrain and the higher the volume of climbing then the greater this consumption becomes. As a general guide the runner should consume about 30 grams of carbohydrate every hour which equates to around 150 calories or in layman's terms about half of a Snickers or Mars bar.

During the course of Day 1 this energy is taken on-board in the form of snacks eaten while on the run or during very short breaks taken from running. When eating on the run take advantage of those moments where you are unable to have a fast forward momentum such as walking up a hill or walking over rough ground. Save the fast moving sections for running.
A typical menu for each runner during Day 1 will be along the lines of:
1 x banana.
4 x energy bars of differing flavours.
1 x sandwich probably of something like jam and peanut butter.
1 x pack of jelly babies or dried fruit.

The banana is a well recognised source of slow-release carbohydrate and that coupled with the jam and peanut butter sandwich, which contains fat and protein, makes a well-balanced light meal during a quick break around the middle of the day. It also gives a change from the energy bars, something which can come as a welcome relief.

Energy bars speak for themselves, they contain a mixture of fast and slow release energy and are designed to keep you going over a period of prolonged exercise. There are a number of different makes and flavours on the market so there is quite a range of choice available. However be aware that some makes and/or flavours may not necessarily suit everybody's stomach. Its always best to experiment with these long before the event, on the marathon always use a make and flavour of energy bar with which you are familiar and accustomed. Try and take a mixture of flavours, it breaks the monotony of eating the same thing all the time.

The majority of the food taken is fairly slow release energy, however, at times it may become necessary to eat something that provides a quick release of sugar into the system just to give that quick kick of energy. Items along the lines of jelly babies or dried fruit provides that sugar rush and can be snacked on at any point during the run.

Regular breaks to take on energy and fluid can, in the long run, be more time effective than pushing yourself to the point of exhaustion before you stop for a break. Taking shelter behind a wall or something similar will also help to conserve energy as the body will not be using reserves fighting the elements.

17.4 Over-night.

At the overnight camp the priority is to get the tent up first in order to provide you with some shelter and then to get some food and drink inside you.

While you are setting up the tent and the cooking equipment you can be snacking on any remaining energy bars or other snippets remaining from the Day 1 running food. Once you are set-up concentrate on getting the evening meal prepared and eaten.

Evening meal.

With the overnight meal there is a two-pronged aim:
1. To replenish the carbohydrates used during the course of the day; and
2. To carbo-load for the following day.

Whichever type of food that you have decided to eat, make sure that it is rich in carbohydrate. One of the advantages of using the commercially available expedition food is that it is already prepared in a high-carb format and you don't have to worry about assembling the meal yourself and making sure that you

And tonight's evening meal is ....

have the right balance. Forget any diets and take a pudding, the more calories that you can get into you the better, you'll wear it off the following day. The mountain marathoner who weighs more at the end of the event than they did at the start is yet to be born.

On the luxury side it is always worthwhile taking yourself a little treat and it also provides a welcome change from the day's food. Perhaps a chocolate bar of some kind although a number of people do advocate a small packet of peanuts which also contain salt, fat and protein, all useful after a hard day's exercise.

Tip. If you think that the cooked meal is not going to be sufficient then consider taking additional food that doesn't need to be cooked such as cheese, biscuits, dried fruit etc.

Breakfast.
Porridge is a great favourite with the mountain marathon fraternity. It is easy to prepare, especially the boiling-water-in-the-bag variety, and it is a good source of slow release carbohydrate to fuel the day's running. Other alternatives are other forms of cereal and/or breakfast bars and occasionally you will see teams frying up the full English.

Don't forget, when eating both the evening meal and breakfast continue to constantly take on small volumes of fluid. It is one of these Catch-22 situations, carbohydrate can't be stored in the body without absorbing fluids and fluids can't be stored in the body without absorbed carbohydrate.

17.5 During the second day of the event.
The second day of the event is very much the same as the first with energy maintenance being a high priority. Unfortunately by the time the second day comes round any of the real tasty but more perishable snacks from the first day will have been long consumed leaving just energy bars and any remaining jelly babies or dried fruit.

The routine of eating on the run will be just the same as on Day 1 even though the second day will tend to be slightly shorter.

Due to the shorter day you would probably get away with just three energy bars over the course of the day. However, it may be advisable to carry four keeping one as a spare in case the need arrives. If not used it will probably get eaten on the way home.

Be aware that with some mountain marathons you are required to have some food left over at the end of the marathon as "emergency food" and you may be asked to produce this.

17.6 Post event and recovery.

After you have passed through the finishing line most events have some form of post-event catering supplying a meal to help kick-start the recovery process. The nature and volume of this meal varies from event to event but it is always wise to have something in your car ready for you to start nibbling at anyway. Try and make this as different from the dehydrated food that you have been eating over the weekend as possible otherwise it may just not seem attractive enough to eat.

More details on eating after the event and during the recovery period are included in the section After the Event.

18. Hydration.

Don't underestimate the effects that fluid intake or more accurately lack of fluid intake can have on your performance. All endurance activities can be curtailed by insufficient drinking and this is a serious factor to consider in an event that spans two days. Remember thirst develops when the body is 5% dehydrated and a fall in the body's fluid levels by this 5% does have the potential to reduce your exercise capacity by up to a staggering 20%.

This chapter looks at the need to drink, what you should drink and the practical aspects of getting enough fluid into your body.

18.1 Selecting your drinks.
The two main factors that contribute to fatigue during any exercise are:
1. Dehydration through a loss of fluid as a result of sweating, and
2. The depletion of the body's carbohydrate stores.

Electrolyte drinks
Electrolyte drinks are for endurance runs and hot weather. As the body sweats it loses electrolytes (salts and minerals) and this can lead to dehydration within the muscle cells, muscle fatigue and damage. These drinks are designed to be taken with water and are aimed at replacing this electrolyte loss. They do not contain energy.

Energy drinks
Energy drinks are normally a mix of various carbohydrates such as maltodextrin, fructose and glucose. They replenish the body's glycogen stores within the muscles. Being a drink they are useful for activities where eating is difficult such as running. Care needs to be taken with these as if consumed on their own they can cause dehydration, so they need to be taken along with plenty of water.

For a mountain marathoner out on the hill for up to eight hours per day for two consecutive days then the primary drink is going to be water and lots of it. Sufficient water will help prevent dehydration but water on it's own cannot replace the electrolytes lost through sweating nor can it replace the body's carbohydrate stores. For that you then need to look at sports drinks and using them during your competition weekend.

Electrolyte and energy drinks are quite often called hypotonic, isotonic and hypertonic which all adds to the confusion. Essentially:

1. Hypotonic drinks are designed to maintain hydration and are an electrolyte drink.
2. Isotonic drinks provide both electrolytes and also carbohydrate and so provide a cross between electrolyte and energy drinks.
3. Hypertonic drinks supply carbohydrate and rarely contain any electrolytes and so are purely energy drinks.

18.2 Pre-event.

Drinking during the event is one thing but as with making sure your energy levels are high before the event it is also worthwhile making sure that you are fully hydrated when you stand on the start line. This will involve drinking during the period before the race and also during the couple of hours on race day that lead up to the start.

The days before the marathon.

On the three or four days before the event increase your drink intake to a higher than normal amount in order to increase the fluid level in your body. Any excess consumed will just end up being pee'd out although you might get sick of going to the loo. The way to tell when you are fully hydrated is when your pee is both clear and in large volume.

On the morning prior to the start.

With most mountain marathons there is normally a lengthy journey to the event which for most competitors will mean travelling the day before and then camping at the event centre over night. Even though camping, it is important to keep the hydration levels high overnight and into the morning of the event. Continue drinking little but often.

One aspect that is often forgotten on these events is the walk to the start. It is not unknown for this to take twenty or thirty minutes and with some events this may even involve some form of transportation to the start. Then there is the standing around waiting for your start time which can also be quite lengthy. Carry additional drinks to consume during this time. Don't use the drinks that you have actually prepared for the run itself. Any empty bottles can sometimes be left at the start, however, it is always best to check with the organisers on this as facilities at some events may be limited.

18.3 During the first day of the event.

Drinking on the Run.

Dependent upon class and whether you have any navigation "incidents" or not, you can be out on the hillside for up to eight hours on Day 1 and almost as long on Day 2. This level of exercise does require sufficient hydration and that means drinking often and regularly. For prolonged periods of activity like this, it is normally suggested drinking every twenty minutes or so as the ideal, however, if running in high temperatures you may find that there is a need to drink more often.

This drinking every twenty minutes is, as said above, the ideal situation however this is an extremely short time interval between drinks especially while you are navigating a leg or when you are trying to optimise a fast running section. In reality you will find that in some cases it will be hard to stick to a twenty minute schedule and you will be just drinking whenever you can, so you may have the situation where you are drinking every twenty minutes and then have a gap of thirty or forty minutes before the next drink. Use the following as a guideline:

1. Every 20 minutes - the ideal preferred option drinking small quantities each time.

2. Every 40 minutes - in some cases and on some legs that have complex navigation and/or fast moving sections this may be the more realistic option, you will find that by the time 40 minutes is up you will be feeling thirsty and you will consume a larger volume than on the 20 minute option.

3. Every 60 minutes - the worst case scenario, by the time 60 minutes is up you will be feeling very thirsty and when you do drink you will tend to gulp back quite a large volume of liquid which has the potential to cause stomach cramps resulting in lost time while you recover.

4. Over 60 minutes - never go longer than 60 minutes without taking fluid on board.

Drink small quantities at regular intervals or as regular as you can get during the course of the run. Don't wait until you are feeling thirsty. Remember the simple fact .... if you are feeling thirsty then it is already too late and you are on the way to becoming dehydrated.

Practicalities of drinking on the run.

Drinking even small quantities on this regular basis does add up to a considerable volume of water for a day's needs, far too much to actually carry while out on the event. This does mean having to find suitable sources of drinking water while you are out on the course and, in addition, as you can not rely on finding a stream every time that you need a drink, having to carry a container in which to transport these fluids so that you can drink between streams.

A well-tried method that is adopted by a number of runners is the carrying of two 500 ml drinks bottles. Start the event with both of these bottles full and as you run consume the contents of one of the bottles. When that bottle is empty, obviously then start on the contents of the second bottle and while doing so top up the empty first bottle at the first available source of water. Follow this pattern of always filling your empty bottle while still having available drink in your second bottle, this ensures that you always have drinks and always top up the empty bottle at the first opportunity. Don't work on the assumption that a stream may turn up in the next half mile or so, at some point it wouldn't and you could be left with no drinks for a lengthy time.

As an alternative to carrying drinks bottles many rucksacks now have a self-contained drinks bladder, the capacity of which can vary from model to

Take the opportunity to top your drinks bottles up at every chance as the opportunity to do this may not necessarily happen on a regular basis. This applies even more so during warm weather when the threat of dehydration is higher whilst at the same time the chance of finding suitable running water will be much reduced.

model. If you choose this option make sure that the bladder is easy to remove and refill during the course of the run.

A number of the elite athletes carry no water with them at all, just a light plastic mug which is used for drinking out of streams as they pass them.

Tip. Don't always wait until your drinks bottles or bladder are empty to top them up. Use common sense and if it looks as if you are about to run over a long stretch where finding a water source may be difficult then fill your bottles as and when water is available even if they are not empty yet.

Finding water while out on the run.
Mountain marathons are a test of navigational ability so therefore it is fair to assume that you can identify a water source from a map, the clue is that they are normally blue. However careful looking at the map will also tell you, in most cases, whether the water source is running water or still water. The preferred option is to always go for running water, still water has a higher chance of being stagnant and unhealthy.

Being an island and a relatively wet one at that, it is rare where your route does not cross water at least once on any single navigational leg. Occasionally you may have to make a slight diversion to pick up a suitable stream but that would not normally be anything drastic. However that being said, there may be occasions during hot weather where there may be a need to deliberately plot your route away from the best line in order to meet a suitable stream. In these weather conditions fluid intake then becomes a matter of race tactics and the choice needs to be made over lost time and the need to keep fluid levels high to benefit longer term performance.

Where to look for water.
1. The higher you go, the less risk of pollution. Check out the contours to see whether you are high enough to avoid the bad stuff.

2. Avoid places down stream of a path. People will be walking through the water disturbing the sediment and possibly having dirty footwear.

3. Avoid streams that have tributaries. Instead use these tributaries to go higher up and lessen the risks.

4. Look for moving water, don't use static pools. The still water collects organic sediment and can be a breeding ground for pathogens.

5. Avoid places downstream from a tarn, campsite or even old workings such as mine entrances. Other people on the fell may have washed in the water or possibly worse.

6. Keep an eye out for farms or other sites of human habitation. These often have animals plus septic tanks, both of which can leak contaminants into the water supply.

What can get you.

There are three types of water-borne pathogen that can get you:

1. Virus
2. Bacteria
3. Parasites.

Of these the most commonly picked up are:

1. Streptococcus
A bacteria. To eliminate: boil, filter or disinfect.

2. E. coli
A bacteria. To eliminate: boil, filter or disinfect.

3. Giardia Lamblia
A parasite. To eliminate: boil, filter or disinfect.

4. Cryptosporidium.
Close cousin of the malaria parasite. To eliminate: boil and micro filtration. It can be resistant to chemical disinfections.

5. Rotavirus
A virus. To eliminate: boil and disinfection. Not removed by filtration.

How to clean potentially contaminated water.

Water purification.
This is personal preference, some people have no objection with drinking direct from a stream while others would never contemplate it in a thousand years. To some degree this will depend on the type of terrain that the event will be running over and whether you would be encountering clear mountain streams or muddy peat bogs. However be aware that drinking any untreated water, irrespective of its source, does always carry the potential for some health risk.

There are a number of alternative methods of water purification, some more effective than others and some that take longer than others. Generally the more effective methods take longer to work and in the atmosphere of a competitive event you are then faced with the decision of time versus effectiveness. A number of the more common methods of water purification are listed below.

Boiling
Boiling kills all water-borne pathogens and is the safest way to purify water. The organisms carried in water will all start to die off around 55-60 degrees C. Rising steam and bubbling for a few minutes is a good indicator that the water will be safe to drink. While this may be a good option for the overnight camp, it is a little bit impractical during the heat of the competition on Days 1 and 2.

Filtering
Filtering is a good way of cleaning water as it is fast and also removes particles of earth and grit. Most water filters are capable of removing bacteria and parasites but aren't effective against viruses which are too small for the filters to sift.

Chemical disinfection
Chemical disinfection with chlorine tablets is effective against bacteria, parasites and viruses but doesn't work against cryptosporidium. This method does leave an unpleasant taste in the water and can take a while to work.

Also available nowadays are filter bottles which are drinking bottles with in-built filters to remove bacteria and solids. Some makes and models also include filters that are effective against the majority of viruses.

The steripen is a lightweight device that uses ultraviolet light to purify water from microbes very quickly and easily.

Tip. Before taking water from a stream always have a quick look upstream in case of dead sheep or other obvious contaminants.

Prepacked energy drinks.
Irrespective of your personal preference in energy drinks if possible always go for the powder type that can be mixed with water. Prior to the event pre-measured quantities can then be measured out into small plastic bags to be carried on the event. Pre-measuring the quantity of powder ensures that the correct concentration of the mix is maintained and optimum use made of the energy drink. As you fill your water bottle at a stream, a bag of powder can then be added and allowed to dissolve while you are consuming the contents of your still full bottle.

A further tip is to carry a couple of spare bags of powder for the overnight camp. There is nothing to stop the contents of a bag or two being tipped into the stew pot, at this point in the event the taste is only of secondary importance.

Drinking during training.

Maintaining the correct fluid levels in your body has a crucial effect on your performance, see "The effects of insufficient fluids in the body" below. As such a similar drinking regime as you would expect to use during the event should also be used during your long training in preparation for the marathon.

1. Practising not only the physical side of taking drinks but also the mental aspects such as instinctively knowing when to drink, planning routes in order to find drinking water etc will make subtle improvements in your event performance.

2. Training while impaired through lack of fluids will not give you the optimum preparation for the marathon. Adequate fluid intake will ensure that you get the most benefit from the training phase.

18.4 Over-night.

Rehydration.

Irrespective of how much you have drunk during Day 1 by the time that you arrive at the overnight camp it is fairly certain that you will be suffering from dehydration to some degree. Quite simply the overnight camp is where you need to rest, put back calories and rehydrate ready for the next day.

Rehydrating is just putting back as much fluid into the body as you can and that means constantly drinking. Again use common sense, don't drink two gallons of water as soon as you finish, as always, it is a case of little but often. The practical measure of whether you are absorbing sufficient fluid is going to be your urine in so far as, have you drunk enough to go and when you do, what colour is it. As most people know dehydration causes a concentration of minerals in the urine resulting in it becoming a deeper yellow colour. To ensure adequate rehydration you need to drink enough so that you start to go on a regular basis and that your pee becomes clear. At this stage you have a sufficient volume of fluid flushing through the system.

What do you drink.

Basically anything that you can get your hands on. You may have some rehydration drink with you either in liquid or powder form and then most people will drink tea, coffee or powered chocolate drink. Don't worry about tea or coffee being diuretic, the volume of liquid actually in the drink will more than compensate for that fluid lost.

Amidst all these other drinks don't forget about plain water. Keep topping on this as well.

Constant drinking overnight, small regular quantities, helps to ensure a speedy return to normal hydration levels.

Some events, notably the Saunders, have facilities where you can buy milk or beer at the overnight camp. As long as you don't overdo it on the beer, a pint or two shouldn't cause any detrimental effect on your running the next day and as with tea and coffee above, the diuretic effect will be mitigated by the volume of fluid in the drink.

Facilities at the overnight site.
This very much depends on event and location. Some events have a water supply laid on at the camp either by standpipe or by bowser. Other events rely on a stream running past the campsite to supply the water. There is no hard and fast rule on this and some events will move from having a supplied source to a streamed source from year to year dependant upon the remoteness of the campsite.

If the water source is from a stream then be very careful not to contaminate the water for fellow competitors. Do activities such as cleaning your teeth and washing pots and pans downstream from the point where the drinking water is being collected. It goes without saying that you should not be urinating or

Sourcing drinking water from a stream at the overnight camp.

defecating anywhere near the stream or for that matter anywhere on the campsite, that is what the portaloos are there for.

Practicalities.
Most competitors carry dehydrated food and dehydrated drink for the overnight stay. This obviously requires water to prepare plus you will also require water to drink, this is a considerable volume of water and you don't necessarily want to be trotting backwards and forwards to the taps or stream with your little 500 ml bottles. Many competitors carry a collapsible plastic container to carry and store the water in. This can be the inside of a wine box or a commercially available product.

18.5 During the second day of the event.
Very similar to Day 1 however you do need to be aware that you may already be starting the day's activities already leaning towards dehydration due to the previous day's exertions especially if you haven't rehydrated sufficiently overnight. Don't be surprised if you do feel the need to drink more than you did on Day 1.

Also as the day progresses the excitement or panic of finishing the event, dependent on how well you think that you have done, can start to mount and it can be very easy to start to forget or neglect to take in sufficient fluid. Make sure that you stick to your drinks regime as much as possible.

18.6 Post event and recovery.

As with the end of Day 1, by the time you finish Day 2 you will be dehydrated and just as it is at the overnight camp, it is important to get fluids into the body as soon as possible. Whether you stay for the post-race meal or head for home straight away, keep drinking small quantities on a regular basis. If you are driving home then plan your journey to give plenty of breaks to enable you to take on fluid.

The same principle holds for the following few days after the marathon. Keep your fluid intake at a higher rate than normal for a couple of days after the event. The sooner that your body is restored to it's normal capacity and that includes hydration levels then the sooner that you will be able to return to normal training.

Tip. After the event don't go back to the normal tea and coffee levels, keep a high water intake even for just a few days.

18.7 The effects of insufficient fluids in the body.

Exercise produces heat within the body and unless this heat is removed this can lead to significant increases in the body's core temperature. To remove this heat the body sweats but if the fluid lost as sweat is not replaced then dehydration will occur and the body temperature will increase anyway.

Dehydration by as little as 2% of your body mass can have a dramatic effect on both mental and physical performance.

The mental aspect will affect your ability to navigate.
1. You will find it hard to concentrate, route planning and observing landmarks as you pass them will become difficult.
2. Your ability to focus will diminish as will your ability to make decisions.
3. Your reaction time will get slower and so will affect your responses to running over rough ground.

On the physical side.
4. Being dehydrated will hasten on the feelings of fatigue and your physical performance will deteriorate.
5. Your average running speed will become slower and rest breaks will become more regular.
6. Your muscles will start to ache and become sore much sooner than what you are normally accustomed to.

TRAINING.

Completing a mountain marathon over two days in mountainous terrain is obviously a serious physical challenge no matter which level of class that you aim for and requires a corresponding degree of physical fitness. This section looks at how to prepare to meet this challenge.

The first chapter of the section looks at the demands and the requirements of training for this kind of event. The second chapter presents a series of suggested training schedules to follow during this training. The third looks at the practicalities of running over rough terrain with a fully laden rucksack. The last sets out an annual training guide for those wanting to compete in more than one event a year.

Navigation training - a fundamental part of any training program for the mountain marathon.

19. Training for the Event.

This first chapter of the section looks at the demands and the requirements of training for this kind of event. The second part presents a series of suggested training schedules to follow during this training.

19.1 Training needs.
The first rule of all training is to make that training appropriate for the event. With a mountain marathon being comprised of long-distance endurance running while navigating your way over rough, mountainous terrain then it should come as no surprise that your training should include all the elements that will improve your ability to run long-distances while navigating over rough, mountainous terrain.

Due to its nature this will include having to perform training sessions over similar rough, mountainous terrain as you would encounter on the marathon and you will need to get out there in the hills and practice these sessions and do this on a regular basis.

Below, you will find a breakdown of all the elements that will need to be reflected in your training. Attention to each of these will improve your ability to get round one of these marathons, failure to include each of these aspects may not actually stop you getting round but it will certainly make it more painful.

19.2 Length of training period.
The length of training period chosen for the training schedules below is 30 weeks. For those who are new to mountain marathon training this period has been selected as being the most appropriate to become accustomed to the demands and fatigues of this type of training. This allows for a slow build-up from a fairly moderate training base up to a relatively high training level while still leaving sufficient time to allow an adequate taper or recovery in the weeks leading to the event.

For the more experienced runner who has a background in this type of demanding running it is possible to drop into the schedules at an appropriate point and then complete the rest of the schedule.

19.3 Planning your training.

As can be seen from the sections below there are many constituent parts to training for a mountain marathon which range through hill work to endurance and navigational training. To ensure your best possible performance in the event, all of these areas need to be worked on and, as importantly, included within your training.

Unfortunately improving your performance does not come overnight and the preparation for a mountain marathon is more of a long-term goal than a short-term fix. As a result it becomes essential to prepare a well-balanced training plan, it is far too easy to train haphazardly especially when it is being done over a longer time period where the focus can easily drift and be lost. Your training needs to be structured into a set laid-down plan that is both easy to follow and to stick to. This will also help to ensure that over the training period all of the constituent parts are included and that none become ignored or neglected.

This approach is reflected within the suggested training schedules included below, here a balanced plan has been built-up to incorporate all the elements necessary to improve your performance over a mountain marathon.

19.4 Training patterns

One of the unique characteristics of mountain marathons is the fact that it is a two day competition with a substantial distance being run on Day 1 and just slightly less, ran on Day 2. The actual distances covered will depend on class entered and route choice.

This gives the running pattern of two long days of up to six hours per day, one after the other. As most endurance runners have a training pattern consisting of a long endurance run just then one day per week normally on the Sunday, preparing to run two long distances on two consecutive days by only running a long distance on just the one day obviously leaves something missing.

One of the fundamentals of training is specificity; the best training is that which is specific to the event that you are competing in. Therefore it is logical to train over a two day period in a manner that is similar to that experienced during the marathon. Whereas there is no doubt that you could complete a mountain marathon based on just the one long run per week, a significant improvement in your performance would be achieved by mirroring the actual running pattern within your training schedule and complete two long training runs over two days, one after the other.

If, prior to training for the mountain marathon, you have not actually run two long days in succession then to assist in building up to this level of training perform your run on the first day during the early morning and on the second day in the late afternoon/evening. During the initial period of training this will allow a greater recovery period between the two runs. This can then be adjusted by moving the time of the second day's run closer to the early morning and so replicating the running pattern found on the actual event.

To that end, the suggested training schedules included below have a number of sessions where long distances are run on two consecutive days

19.5 Endurance training.

The mountain marathon is a predominantly endurance based event and so all training will be based on increasing your ability to maintain movement over a long period of time. As the aim is navigation and finding your own route across open country, there is no fixed distance that has to be travelled in order to complete the event. This distance will depend upon the nature of the terrain plus

The mountain marathon is an endurance based activity and at the end of the day there is no substitute for long endurance runs carrying full equipment and ran over suitable terrain. It is the only way to fully prepare.

your own route finding ability and the distance travelled even by competitors on the same course will vary.

Distance covered during training then becomes rather meaningless and a more accurate determiner of the training effect is time on your feet, i.e. running for a specific time period. As can be seen from the training schedules, as the initial training phase is performed mileage is used as the determiner to the aim of the session as the schedule then moves more into the core training then this changes and the determiner becomes running for a specific length of time. At the end of this period, as the taper phase of the schedule is moved into then once again the determiner becomes running over a specific distance.

19.6 Uphill training.

As the name mountain marathon suggests, a considerable amount of going up and coming down hills occurs on these events. The competitor therefore has to have the strength and endurance necessary to meet the significant demands that they are likely to meet. Hill reps are included within this schedule to obtain and strengthen this ability.

The reps themselves will be graded by total height gained and it is assumed that the runner following this schedule will have the necessary terrain available on which to train, for example a hill session of six reps of 500 feet of climbing. However if this is not possible then, although not as effective, a session comprised of more reps of less height will be adequate, for example thirty reps of 100 feet of climbing will still give you a total climb of 3,000 feet.

Part of the climbing in these events could be quite steep which when combined with carrying a heavy load will enforce, at times, walking up the slope. To replicate this some of the hill reps will be expected to include very steep sections forcing you to walk.

As with most events over open fell and mountain terrain, being able to climb the necessary height is not the full picture and the location of the climbs within the race route can be very relevant as, for example, a steep climb ten miles into a race when exhaustion has started to set in can be very testing. To condition for this why not include within some of your longer training a small hill rep session at some point within the run.

19.7 Downhill training.

As mentioned in Uphill training above, there can be a substantial amount of descending on one of these events and in some cases individual descents can be quite prolonged in terms of distance. Such large volumes of descending can put heavy strains on the muscles of the leg especially when carrying a heavily-laden rucksack as this effectively increases the body weight and the resulting impact stress.

Couple this with the fact that the majority of the descents would be down over rocky paths, tussock grass and other uneven surfaces plus usually a large proportion of the descending is in the final stages of the race when an element of fatigue has set in and the probability to make mistakes leading to strained ankles and other injuries becomes quite high.

Downhill reps have been included as part of the training plan in order to condition the body to meet these demands including some sessions over relatively rough terrain. As with the uphill sessions above, why not include a small session partway through a long run.

19.8 Speed training.

Being predominantly endurance based the requirement for a mountain marathon is for speed endurance, that is being able to maintain a relatively high speed for as long as possible. However what does need to be borne in mind is that speed is relative and what would be considered as high speed during a mountain marathon would be relatively slow in comparison to that for an equivalent ten mile race.

But what is not generally realised, is that speed sessions in the form of interval and repetition runs can also be used to develop the endurance ability. To this end the bulk of the speed training sessions included below are over the more longer-based distances in order to increase these abilities.

A number of shorter, faster paced sessions have also been included in order to help increase basic running speed which the longer sessions will help prolong.

Some of the speed sessions can be done on an athletics track or on road/pavement to enable a faster pace to be built-up if desired. However, most sessions have been deliberately staged on off-road terrain such as forest road or track to help become accustomed to faster-paced running on similar terrain over which the race is held.

Recovery between individual reps is given as within the training sessions. Timings do not have to be down to the exact second.

19.9 Terrain training.

All mountain marathons are going to be run over a variety of terrain ranging from stony paths and hard-packed tracks to open moorland complete with heather bashing and bog hopping. As a result slightly different running styles will need to be adopted during these different stages of the event as you change from one type of terrain to another. Training runs do need to be performed over the appropriate terrain in order to help the body adapt to the resulting different stresses that will be placed on it. Whenever possible terrain similar to that which could be expected in the event should be used during some of your training runs and especially on the longer weekend runs. In addition some of the training sessions in the schedules below have been set to help the body become accustomed to running over this changing terrain.

One vital aspect of terrain training is developing the ability to effectively contour round the side of a hill. Basically contouring is maintaining the same height as you run across the slope. Physically this is difficult due to the fact that as you run across the slope, one leg is always going to be higher than the other.

Contouring round a hillside, a vital skill when competing and navigating in mountain marathons and one that should take a high priority during your long training runs.

Plus there is the mental difficulty in maintaining height as the natural tendency is always going to be to drift down the slope. Contouring needs to be practised just like any other aspect of your training.

19.10 Strength training.

As with all running disciplines there is an element of strength work required during the process of running, after all you are picking up a heavy weight, your body, and propelling it through the air to a point a short distance away. The running stride is effectively a short long jump.

Couple that with the need to carry your full equipment for two days, this means that your bodyweight is heavier than normal, plus you have the additional demands from running over rough terrain and now you can start to see that there is a considerable strength element required for competing in mountain marathons. Having said that it must be pointed out that this strength aspect is actually targeted at the specific needs of the mountain marathon and not something that is more akin to bodybuilding.

Most runners do not see the need for specific strength training and their training is all based around running itself. That is fine and there is no problem with that as running itself is a strength building activity albeit a specific one aimed at developing the muscles that work while running.

However, the majority of runners would benefit from incorporating some level of strength work into their training. Strength training can take several forms, the most used being:
1. Gym work using weights machines.
2. Free weights such as barbells and dumbbells.
3. Circuit training.

If using weight machines and/or free weights it is always advisable to do this, initially at least, under the guidance of a qualified strength and conditioning coach.

Circuit training, using the body's own weight as the resistance rather than an external weight such as a barbell, is an easy and convenient method of developing strength. It does not need any additional equipment and can be done in the convenience of your own home.

A suitable home circuit training session is included within the training schedules later in this section.

19.11 Flexibility training.

A good flexibility programme for a mountain marathon runner would encompass two distinct purposes.

1. To maintain flexibility and help injury prevention.
2. To improve flexibility and thus increase performance capability.

All the obvious major muscle groups in the legs should be included but in order to meet the peculiar demands of mountain marathons both upper body and especially core (trunk) exercises should also be incorporated into any routine. Carrying loads in a rucksack while running does place strains and stresses on both the upper body and the trunk that do not materialise during more mainstream running disciplines.

More details on stretching and a couple of basic stretching routines are illustrated at the end of this section.

19.12 Recovery.

It is impossible to train at full intensity continuously, at some point the body will breakdown resulting in deteriorating performance and, in the worse case scenario, injury. Recovery phases and sessions have been built into this training plan to enable both the body and the mind to rest and recover from the exertions caused by hard training. They are planned to give a balanced training schedule and to enable the runner to maintain optimum training intensity throughout the schedule and should be followed and not be ignored because "I feel like doing a harder session". However if at any point you feel the need for additional rest or to throttle back on any particular session then do so. It is much better to miss a session than to force hard work when fatigued.

When used, recovery runs should be performed at the slowest possible pace so that muscles will be loosened through exercise but not that fast where lactate will be generated and muscles will be strained.

19.13 Night training.

The first day of any mountain marathon can be a long day, even longer if you have some navigational mishaps. During the summer events when you have the long, light summer evenings this doesn't tend to present any problems. However, in events during the back end of the year when the nights start cutting-in then this does mean that there is the possibility of finishing the first day just as dusk is falling or even, in the worst case, in the dark.

For those who have never or rarely ran and navigated under these circumstances then this can be a little bit unnerving and for some people can even cause a mild element of panic. If you think that there may be a possibility of you being caught out this way then it may be advisable to do some preparation by including some running at night with the use of a headtorch. This will help familiarise yourself with the feel of being out on the fell in the dark.

You don't have to spend hours running across the hills in the pitch black struggling to find your way only with the illumination from a small headtorch. The intention is not to become an expert night runner but rather to do just enough so that you are comfortable with the dark and that panic doesn't set in if this situation does arise.

In the first instance any night training should be done over an area with which you are familiar, you can then start to get the feel of how different the dark can make things seem. As you become more comfortable you can then start to move to areas where you are less familiar and if time permits, ultimately, to an area that would be similar to the competition area.

19.14 Navigation training.
The ability to navigate is one of the fundamental skills required to complete a mountain marathon. Whereas navigation techniques are outside the scope of this book, see our sister book "Navigation for Off-Road Runners", it is essential to practice these skills during your training for this event. As you'll see from the suggested training schedules further down, regular long weekend runs are used to help build up endurance capacity and it would make sense to use a proportion of these runs to practice these techniques especially if the training run is being held over similar terrain to that which will be encountered during the event. In effect you would be treating these long runs as a form of mini-marathon practising and training both endurance and navigation.

20. Training Schedules.

In the following pages are three training schedules to cater for three different classes of competition:
Team 1. Classes A, elite and long score.
Team 2. Classes B and medium score.
Team 3. Classes C and short score.

In the booklet "Mountain Marathon Preparation" we looked at club runners who focussed on mileage per week and wanted to "just" complete a mountain marathon safely. In the three schedules that follow we aim to expand on that principle and these schedules are aimed at those runners who seek the improve their performance.

The schedules are based on a 30 week training program leading up to the marathon and the training is based on the following principle:
Week 30 to week 22. Transition training.
Week 23 to week 16. General base training.
Week 15 to week 8. Specific base training.
Week 7 to week 3. Pre-competition training.
Week 2 to week 1. Competition training.

Assumptions.

1. The runner will enter these schedules with a base running capacity of at least 25, 20 or 15 miles per week for teams 1, 2 and 3 respectively.

2. Each session within the schedule should include a warm-up and cool-down period.

Within each individual schedule:

1. As the schedule moves from the general base training to the specific base training in week 16 you'll notice that the emphasise for the long run moves from miles to hours. This is to reflect the number of hours that you will be on your feet during the course of the event. When the training enters the competition phase the emphasis will again move back to mileage as the training tapers off to ensure full recovery before the marathon.

2. One session per week is recorded as "session" and this follows a specific, structured, weekly training session such as hill reps, fartlek and terrain training. A table detailing each individual session is included at the end of the schedules.

3. During the course of the training regular sessions are given over to "X-train". These are sessions that are given over to developing the necessary strength required for the training program. The sessions themselves will consist of strength and conditioning or circuit training. As with the sessions above these are detailed at the end of the schedules.

4. Also included within the schedules are regular rest periods. The basic concept behind all training is to put the body under a slightly higher degree of pressure than is usual and then to rest it. It is while the body is going through this rest and recovery part of the training that it actually adapts and becomes accustomed to this higher level of pressure and not during the hard training itself. So as you can see, it is vital to include a well-balanced period of rest into any training schedule during which the benefit of the hard training takes affect.

For the majority of competitors the term "rest" will mean exactly that, a day off from training. However for those experienced runners accustomed to a high mileage then the term "rest" could refer to a slow, easy 2 or 3 mile run where the body is just ticking over without any undue stress placed on it.

20.1 TEAM 1 Classes A, Elite and Long Score

Although the distance covered, height climbed and harshness of the terrain will vary dependant upon event and location, the courses for the classes Elite, A and Long Score are considered to be the hardest. Distances covered over the two days generally range from around 55 km to 75 km with a total height gain of between 3,000 and 5,000 foot. However this may not always be the case and it is possible to get a longer distance with a lower height gain and visa versa.

Bear in mind that the distances quoted here are the straight-line distances going from control to control. Poor navigation or route choice can lengthen these distances considerably and can also increase the amount of climbing and descending.

Due to the severity of these courses the competitors can expect to spend a considerable time out on the hill. The long distance runs included within this schedule reflects this.

W/C	Mon	Tues	Wed	Thurs	Fri	Sat	Sun
Week 30	Rest	3 miles	X-train	Session 1	Rest	9 miles	9 miles
Week 29	Rest	4 miles	3 miles	Session 2	Rest	10 miles	10 miles
Week 28	Rest	x-train	4 miles	Session 3	Rest	8 miles	10 miles
Week 27	Rest	4 miles	X-train	Session 10	Rest	9 miles	11 miles
Week 26	Rest	5 miles	4 miles	Session 1	Rest	10 miles	12 miles
Week 25	Rest	x-train	5 miles	Session 2	Rest	9 miles	11 miles
Week 24	Rest	5 miles	X-train	Session 3	Rest	10 miles	12 miles
Week 23	Rest	6 miles	5 miles	Session 10	Rest	11 miles	13 miles
Week 22	Rest	x-train	6 miles	Session 12	Rest	10 miles	12 miles

1. Transition
Weeks 30 to 22

The transition stage is the basic preparation for the endurance training that is to follow, in other words, the preparation of the body to meet the demands of the high volume training to come.

W/C	Mon	Tues	Wed	Thurs	Fri	Sat	Sun
Week 21	Rest	6 miles	X-train	Session 11	Rest	11 miles	13 miles
Week 20	Rest	7 miles	6 miles	Session 4	Rest	12 miles	14 miles
Week 19	Rest	x-train	7 miles	Session 5	Rest	11 miles	13 miles
Week 18	Rest	7 miles	X-train	Session 6	Rest	12 miles	14 miles
Week 17	Rest	8 miles	7 miles	Session 10	Rest	14 miles	16 miles
Week 16	Rest	X-train	5 miles	Session 10	Rest	3 hours	4 hours

2. General base training

Weeks 21 to 16

During this six week period the general base endurance training is carried out, this is to develop the aerobic ability and the capacity to run long prolonged distances off-road.

The main essence of this and all further training is going to be the two long weekend runs. At this point it is not necessary to carry full kit over these runs as the aim is more to prepare you to be capable of running two long distances on consecutive days.

W/C	Mon	Tues	Wed	Thurs	Fri	Sat	Sun
Week 15	Rest	5 miles	5 miles	Session 7	Rest	3 hours	4 hours
Week 14	Rest	X-train	5 miles	Session 8	Rest	4 hours	5 hours
Week 13	Rest	5 miles	5 miles	Session 9	Rest	4 hours	5 hours
Week 12	Rest	X-train	6 miles	Session 11	Rest	5 hours	6 hours
Week 11	Rest	6 miles	6 miles	Session 7	Rest	5 hours	6 hours
Week 10	Rest	X-train	6 miles	Session 8	Rest	6 hours	7 hours
Week 9	Rest	6 miles	6 miles	Session 9	Rest	6 hours	7 hours
Week 8	Rest	X-train	7 miles	Session 11	Rest	7 hours	8 hours

3. Specific base training
Weeks 15 to 8

The emphasis of the training in these eight weeks is to develop specific endurance to compete in a mountain marathon, to be able to run long distances over two consecutive days over rough mountain terrain while carrying a heavy load.

During the majority of the long weekend runs it is expected that the runner carries full mountain marathon equipment and, wherever possible, train over similar terrain to that which will be encountered in the competition area.

W/C	Mon	Tues	Wed	Thurs	Fri	Sat	Sun
Week 7	Rest	7 miles	7 miles	Session 12	Rest	7 hours	8 hours
Week 6	Rest	X-train	7 miles	Session 11	Rest	8 hours	7 hours
Week 5	Rest	8 miles	8 miles	Session 10	Rest	8 hours	6 hours
Week 4	Rest	X -train	8 miles	Session 3 with number of reps reduced to 10.	Rest	7 hours	5 hours
Week 3	Rest	6 miles	5 miles	Session 2 with number of reps reduced to 8.	Rest	8 miles	6 miles

4. Pre-competition

Weeks 7 to 3

At this point the bulk of the endurance training has already been done and this five week period is used to firstly sharpen the body up for the competition and then, secondly, lead into the tapering period running down to the marathon itself. During this tapering the intensity of the sessions is kept in order to maintain and improve the sharpness but the volume gradually reduces as you progress through the tapering.

W/C	Mon	Tues	Wed	Thurs	Fri	Sat	Sun
Week 2	Rest	4 miles	3 miles	Session 1 with number of reps reduced to 4.	Rest	5 miles	4 miles
Week 1	Rest	Rest	3 miles	Rest	Rest	Event	Event

5. Competition

Weeks 2 & 1

In this final two week period just before the event the emphasis is really on allowing the body to rest and recover after all the exertions placed on it during the previous training. The distance and number of runs is drastically reduced down to just enough to maintain the training effect of previous training but not enough to drain the body. At this late stage before the mountain marathon, no beneficial training effect would be gained from any serious training and so the need is to just keep the body sharp and ticking over so that you stand on the start line feeling fresh and raring to go.

20.2 TEAM 2 Classes up to B and Medium Score

As with Team 1 the distances covered and height gained will vary from year to year and location to location. However as a general rule of rule of thumb over the two days the courses will normally cover between 40 and just over 50 km with an ascent of between 2,000 and 3,500 foot of climbing.

In terms of difficulty these courses fall between the more elite classes and the shorter C and short score ones.

The five phases of training used for Team 1 will also apply to Team 2, namely:
Weeks 30 to 22   Transition.
Weeks 21 to 16   General Base Training
Weeks 15 to 8   Specific Base Training
Weeks 7 to 3   Pre-competition
Weeks 2 to 1   Competition

W/C	Mon	Tues	Wed	Thurs	Fri	Sat	Sun
Week 30	Rest	2 miles	X-train	Session 1	Rest	7 miles	7 miles
Week 29	Rest	3 miles	2 miles	Session 2	Rest	8 miles	8 miles
Week 28	Rest	x-train	4 miles	Session 3	Rest	7 miles	8 miles
Week 27	Rest	3 miles	X-train	Session 10	Rest	7 miles	9 miles
Week 26	Rest	4 miles	3 miles	Session 1	Rest	8 miles	10 miles
Week 25	Rest	x-train	4 miles	Session 2	Rest	7 miles	19 miles
Week 24	Rest	4 miles	X-train	Session 3	Rest	8 miles	10 miles
Week 23	Rest	5 miles	4 miles	Session 10	Rest	9 miles	11 miles
Week 22	Rest	x-train	5 miles	Session 12	Rest	8 miles	10 miles

W/C	Mon	Tues	Wed	Thurs	Fri	Sat	Sun
Week 21	Rest	5 miles	X-train	Session 11	Rest	9 miles	11 miles
Week 20	Rest	6 miles	5 miles	Session 4	Rest	10 miles	12 miles
Week 19	Rest	x-train	6 miles	Session 5	Rest	9 miles	9 miles
Week 18	Rest	6 miles	X-train	Session 6	Rest	10 miles	12 miles
Week 17	Rest	7 miles	6 miles	Session 10	Rest	12 miles	14 miles
Week 16	Rest	X-train	4 miles	Session 10	Rest	2 hours	2 hours

W/C	Mon	Tues	Wed	Thurs	Fri	Sat	Sun
Week 15	Rest	4 miles	4 miles	Session 7	Rest	2 hours	4 hours
Week 14	Rest	X-train	4 miles	Session 8	Rest	3 hours	4 hours
Week 13	Rest	4 miles	4 miles	Session 9	Rest	3 hours	5 hours
Week 12	Rest	X-train	5 miles	Session 11	Rest	4 hours	5 hours
Week 11	Rest	5 miles	5 miles	Session 7	Rest	4 hours	6 hours
Week 10	Rest	X-train	5 miles	Session 8	Rest	5 hours	6 hours
Week 9	Rest	5 miles	5 miles	Session 9	Rest	5 hours	7 hours
Week 8	Rest	X-train	6 miles	Session 11	Rest	6 hours	7 hours

W/C	Mon	Tues	Wed	Thurs	Fri	Sat	Sun
Week 7	Rest	6 miles	6 miles	Session 12	Rest	6 hours	7 hours
Week 6	Rest	X-train	6 miles	Session 11	Rest	7 hours	7 hours
Week 5	Rest	7 miles	7 miles	Session 10	Rest	7 hours	7 hours
Week 4	Rest	X-train	7 miles	Session 3 with number of reps reduced to 10.	Rest	6 hours	6 hours
Week 3	Rest	5 miles	4 miles	Session 2 with number of reps reduced to 8.	Rest	7 miles	5 miles

W/C	Mon	Tues	Wed	Thurs	Fri	Sat	Sun
Week 2	Rest	3 miles	2 miles	Session 1 with number of reps reduced to 4.	Rest	4 miles	3 miles
Week 1	Rest	Rest	2 miles	Rest	Rest	Event	Event

20.3 TEAM 3 Classes up to C and Short Score

As with the other classes distance and height will vary from year to year and location to location. With these classes you can assume that over the two days the distance covered will be between 30 and just over 40 km. The total height gained would normally be between 1,500 and just over 3,000 feet. However as with the other two categories exceptions have and will occur from time to time.

The other provisos mentioned under 20.1 Team 1 also apply here.

The five phases of training used for Team 1 will also apply to Team 3, namely:

Weeks 30 to 22   Transition.
Weeks 21 to 16   General Base Training
Weeks 15 to 8   Specific Base Training
Weeks 7 to 3   Pre-competition
Weeks 2 to 1   Competition

W/C	Mon	Tues	Wed	Thurs	Fri	Sat	Sun
Week 30	Rest	1 miles	X-train	Session 1	Rest	5 miles	5 miles
Week 29	Rest	2 miles	1 miles	Session 2	Rest	6 miles	6 miles
Week 28	Rest	x-train	2 miles	Session 3	Rest	4 miles	6 miles
Week 27	Rest	2 miles	X-train	Session 10	Rest	5 miles	7 miles
Week 26	Rest	3 miles	2 miles	Session 1	Rest	6 miles	8 miles
Week 25	Rest	x-train	3 miles	Session 2	Rest	5 miles	7 miles
Week 24	Rest	3 miles	X-train	Session 3	Rest	6 miles	8 miles
Week 23	Rest	4 miles	3 miles	Session 10	Rest	7 miles	8 miles
Week 22	Rest	X-train	4 miles	Session 12	Rest	6 miles	8 miles

W/C	Mon	Tues	Wed	Thurs	Fri	Sat	Sun
Week 21	Rest	4 miles	X-train	Session 11	Rest	7 miles	9 miles
Week 20	Rest	5 miles	5 miles	Session 4	Rest	8 miles	10 miles
Week 19	Rest	x-train	5 miles	Session 5	Rest	7 miles	9 miles
Week 18	Rest	5 miles	X-train	Session 6	Rest	8 miles	10 miles
Week 17	Rest	6 miles	5 miles	Session 10	Rest	10 miles	12 miles
Week 16	Rest	X-train	3 miles	Session 10	Rest	1 hours	3 hours

W/C	Mon	Tues	Wed	Thurs	Fri	Sat	Sun
Week 15	Rest	3 miles	3 miles	Session 7	Rest	1 hours	2 hours
Week 14	Rest	X-train	3 miles	Session 8	Rest	2 hours	1 hours
Week 13	Rest	3 miles	3 miles	Session 9	Rest	1 hours	3 hours
Week 12	Rest	X-train	4 miles	Session 11	Rest	2 hours	3 hours
Week 11	Rest	4 miles	4 miles	Session 7	Rest	2 hours	4 hours
Week 10	Rest	X-train	4 miles	Session 8	Rest	3 hours	4 hours
Week 9	Rest	4 miles	4 miles	Session 9	Rest	3 hours	5 hours
Week 8	Rest	X-train	5 miles	Session 11	Rest	4 hours	5 hours

W/C	Mon	Tues	Wed	Thurs	Fri	Sat	Sun
Week 7	Rest	5 miles	5 miles	Session 12	Rest	4 hours	5 hours
Week 6	Rest	X-train	5 miles	Session 11	Rest	5 hours	5 hours
Week 5	Rest	8 miles	6 miles	Session 10	Rest	5 hours	5 hours
Week 4	Rest	X-train	6 miles	Session 3 with number of reps reduced to 10.	Rest	4 hours	4 hours
Week 3	Rest	4 miles	3 miles	Session 2 with number of reps reduced to 8.	Rest	4 miles	2 miles

W/C	Mon	Tues	Wed	Thurs	Fri	Sat	Sun
Week 2	Rest	2 miles	1 miles	Session 1 with number of reps reduced to 4.	Rest	2 miles	1 miles
Week 1	Rest	Rest	1 miles	Rest	Rest	Event	Event

20.4 Sessions

Details of the individual sessions used within the training schedules are listed below.

Type	Length	Session	Total height gain
1. Speed 2. Uphill 3. Downhill	Short	12 x 100m with 30 sec recovery between each rep.	1,200 to 1,500 feet for the uphill session, the same descent for the downhill session.
4. Speed 5. Uphill 6. Downhill	Medium	10 x 400m with 45 sec recovery between each rep.	2,000 to 3,000 feet for the uphill session, the same descent for the downhill session.
7. Speed 8. Uphill 9. Downhill	Long	8 x 800m with 1 min recovery between each.	3,000 to 3,500 feet for the uphill session, the same descent for the downhill session.
10. Fartlek.	Long	10 km	
11. Terrain	Long	10 km	
12. Speed endurance	Long	Pyramid. 6 reps 100 x 200 x 300 with 1 min recovery between each rep	

In terms of the sessions, for each category of class it may seem unusual performing exactly the same session for an Elite class as it is for a lower C class. However the basic requirements to complete an Elite class are the same as they are to complete a C class. What is relative is the intensity of the various activities, the Elite runner may be doing the same speed session as the C runner but the individual reps would be performed at a faster speed.

The number of the reps built into each session should be no problem irrespective of whether you are running an Elite or a D class course. If you are seriously considering running a mountain marathon then you should be capable of this workload.

Speed sessions are to be held over a relatively flat, stable surface such as a forest track or road, the session can use an undulating surface but the gradients should be gentle and not severe. The purpose of the session is to develop speed and not climbing or descending ability.

Uphill sessions are to be held on an uphill climb for the required distance. Vary the gradients and do not always stick to the same hills. This ensures that you are prepared for the various climbs that you will meet during the course of the event. The uphill session should comprise of a hard uphill effort followed by a gentle downhill jog to recover and get back to the starting position before repeating. On some of the longer uphill reps it may be advisable, at least in part, to include a steep climb that will necessitate some uphill walking.

Downhill sessions are to be held over a downhill descent for the required distance. Vary the gradients and do not always stick to the same hills. This ensures that you are prepared for the various descents that you will meet during the course of the event.

Fartlek is a mixed pace session comprised of a number of legs. After a suitable warm-up, run one leg hard then recover on the next before running hard again on the third leg. Ideally the session should be round an off-road circuit and should include a mixed variety of legs comprised of uphill, downhill and flat running. The legs should also be of a mix of various distances and the overall length of the circuit may be less than the required 10 k but a number of laps may be run to complete the full distance. The primary purpose of this kind of fartlek is to mix speed, uphill and downhill training. Example:

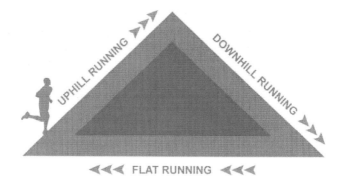

Terrain training is similar to fartlek in so far as it is a session comprised of legs but instead of speed and hill training, it's primary purpose is to condition the body to run effectively over the various types of terrain that you would expect to meet on the event. Ideally each leg should encompass a different type of terrain, for example leg 1 moorland path, leg 2 crossing a heather bed, leg 3 moorland track, etc. Steep uphills and downhills can be included within a terrain session as can such things as streams and river crossings, As with the fartlek session the overall length of the circuit may be less than the required 10k in which case just do the relevant number of laps.

A typical terrain run incorporating a mixture of different ground surfaces is shown below.

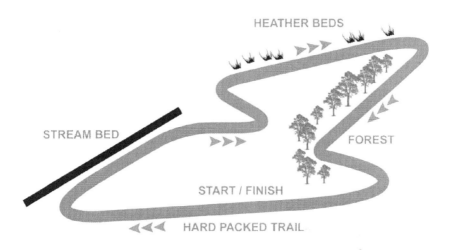

Speed endurance / pyramid session. This type of session uses what are known as pyramids to develop the ability of running fast for long periods hence the name speed endurance. When explained the pyramid session always sounds more complicated than it actually is. From the starting point run 100 metres hard and then do a slow jog / walk recovery back to the start. Then run 200 metres hard before the slow jog / walk back to the start. The third leg would be 300 metres hard before the slow jog / walk recovery. These three runs would comprise the one rep after which you would have the minutes recovery before commencing the second rep. Ideally these should be performed on a surface such as a forest road or other good surface.

20.5 Strength sessions

Below is a simple home-based circuit training session that doesn't use any complicated equipment and is designed to increase the strength of the core muscle groups used during the course of a mountain marathon. Simple exercises can be just as effective as anything more sophisticated and by using your own body weight coupled with a suitable range of movements it is possible to train both the muscle and the range of neuro-muscular connections which can be difficult to do when using fixed-position gym equipment.

One aspect that needs to be borne in mind when training for a mountain marathon is that, unlike in more conventional running events, there is a greater need for both upper and core body strength. This is due to two reasons:

1. The substantial amount of equipment that is carried attached to both the shoulders and trunk of the body, and

2. Also to meet the demands of running over rough terrain with the resulting large amount of movement and twisting that is done by both the trunk and upper body.

The exercises are:

1. Upper body 10 x press-ups.
2. Core 10 x sit-ups.
3. Legs 10 x one-leg squats.
4. Upper body 10 x triceps dips.
5. Core 10 x trunk twists.
6. Legs 10 x calf raise.
7. Overall 10 x burpees.

Perform these exercises with no rest in-between, moving from one exercise to the next. The completion of these would be known as one set. This can be followed by one minutes rest and then repeated by a further set.

Start of with 1 or 2 sets and then increase by 1 set every four weeks to get you up to 4 or 5 sets in total.

Illustrations of the various exercises are below.

1. Upper body 10 x press-ups.
Position the arms slightly wider than shoulder width and lower the body towards the floor before raising again. For those not used to press-ups then they can be performed from the kneeling position.

2. Core 10 x sit-ups.
Lay on the floor with your knees bent and slowly raise your upper body off the ground towards the knees. Keep the hands at the side of the head to stop and possible neck problems when tired.

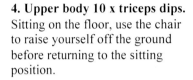

3. Legs 10 x one-leg squats.
Standing on one leg squat down but bend the knee no more than 90 degrees. Complete all the reps with one leg and then repeat with the other leg.

4. Upper body 10 x triceps dips.
Sitting on the floor, use the chair to raise yourself off the ground before returning to the sitting position.

5. Core 10 x trunk twists.
Standing with your feet slightly apart and your arms outstretched, turn from the waist towards the left and then back to the right before returning to the facing ahead position. This counts as one rep.

6. Legs 10 x calf raise.
Standing flat footed on the floor, slowly raise the heels off the ground by balancing on the balls of the feet before returning them to the floor. You may need to use outstretched arms for balance during this exercise.

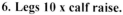

7. Overall 10 x burpees.
From the press-up position, quickly bring your knees up to your arms and then jump into the air. Land and go down into the press-up position again pushing your legs back out behind you. This counts as one rep.

For those with access to and a desire to use free weights in a gym the following sample session can be used. It must always be stressed that for anybody new or inexperienced with the use of weights then expert guidance should be sought from a suitably qualified coach and/or instructor.

Sample free weight session.

Maximum of 3 sets with 1 minute rest between each set.

10 x front squat

10 x lateral raise

10 x leg curls easy

30 x heal raises

10 x back squat

10 x bell curl

20 x cross over jumps (keep the front leg bent and the back leg straight in the lunge position and then jump and while doing so swap the leg positions)

10 x leg curl hard

10 x bar press

For those exercises using dumbbells then the maximum weight used should be no more than 10% of the lifter's body weight.

For those exercises using barbells then the maximum weight used should be no more than 30% of the lifter's body weight.

20.6 Flexibility sessions

Most runners do some form of stretching exercises or if they don't then they know that they should and usually have some level of guilty feelings over missing them out of their routine. The need for stretching was outlined in an earlier section and if you are serious about improving your performance and keeping injuries, niggles and pulls at bay during your training then you should really incorporate, at the minimum, a couple of flexibility sessions per week. These don't have to be anything too structured or involved, ten or fifteen minutes on the front room floor while watching TV would be sufficient.

In terms of exercises performed, the normal runner's stretches involving the calves, quadriceps, hamstrings and gluterals should all be included. However, because of the additional stresses placed on the core and upper body muscles it is also important to include exercises to cover these areas. A couple of days hard exercise over rough terrain while carrying a rucksack and heavy load should convince you.

Illustrated below is a sample stretching routine including several exercises for the core and upper body. All exercises should be moved into slowly and carefully and then held for thirty seconds before release. Never push the exercise to the point where you experience pain, the point is to just feel a gentle stretch within the muscle. If at any time you do experience pain then stop straight away.

Ideally all the exercises should be performed when the muscles are warm such as after gentle exercise. Another alternative is to perform them after the muscles have been warmed in a hot bath.

On the event, by the time you arrive at the overnight camp you could be a bit stiff and sore. Logic would dictate that you should keep moving and perform a mild stretching session to help alleviate this feeling. In practical terms, very few competitors think about doing any stretching once they pass through the final control, the main concern is getting the tent up, getting some food and drink inside them and then flaking out. However, don't flake out straight away, keep moving, have a walk around the camping field, go and get some water for a brew, anything just don't suddenly stop moving. Take a gentle wind-down and, at some point during the evening, try and do some minor exercises such as touching the toes and hamstring stretches. It will help make you feel that little bit better.

Chest Stretch

Stand tall with feet slightly apart. Place your hands, loosely clasped, in the small of your back then keeping your back straight and your shoulders down, try and bring your elbows together. Feel the stretch in the chest muscles.

Upper Back Stretch

Stand tall with the feet slightly apart. Bend your knees slightly, tucking the stomach in. Interlock the fingers, pushing your hands away from the chest, rounding your back and tilting the head to look down at the same time. Feel the stretch between the shoulder blades.

Shoulder and Side Stretch

Stand tall with the feet apart. Raise both arms up and place the hand of the right arm behind the elbow of the left arm to bring the left upper arm behind your head. Repeat with the other arm. Feel the stretch in the shoulder and side of the trunk.

Spine and Trunk Twist

Sit upright on the floor with your legs out in front of you. Bend the right leg to place the right foot on the outside of the left knee. Keeping your shoulders down, twist smoothly round so that the shoulders face forward by using the left elbow as a lever against your right knee and the right arm for balance. Repeat with the other side. Feel the stretch through the trunk, spine and outer thigh.

151

Seated Groin Stretch
Sit upright. Place the soles of the feet together and slowly press your knees towards the floor. Feel the stretch in the inner thighs and the groin area.

Lying Quadriceps Stretch
Lie face down on the floor and bend your left knee up towards your buttocks. Reach round with the left hand to grasp the foot and ease it closer. Repeat on both sides. Feel the stretch in the front of the thigh.

Seated Hamstring Stretch
Sit upright with the legs outstretched. Bend forwards from the waist, slipping the hands down the outside of the legs. Feel the stretch in the backs of the thighs and buttocks and also the lower back.

Back Release
Lie flat on the back and then bring the knees up to the chest, holding them close with your hand. Feel the stretch in the lower back and buttocks.

Lying Hip and Thigh Stretch

Lie flat on your back. Bring the right knee up to your chest, holding it there with your hands while the left leg remains out-stretched. Repeat on both sides. Feel the stretch along the front of the thigh and around the hip.

Hamstring and Groin Stretch

Sit upright with both legs out-stretched. Bend the right leg so that the right foot rests on the inside of the left thigh. Bend forward from the waist to reach for the left foot with your hands. Repeat on both sides. Feel the stretch in the back of the left leg and the groin.

Calf Stretch

Face forward with the hands against a wall at shoulder height, one foot in front of the other. Keeping the back leg straight and pressing the heel on the ground, take it back as far as possible from the wall. Repeat with the other leg. Feel the stretch in the calf.

21. The Effects of Running with a Rucksack and Load.

Mountain marathons are one of the few areas in competitive running where it is compulsory to carry a rucksack with a load. The weight of this load will differ dependent your seriousness as a competitor and how far you go down the route of minimalist weight. However, irrespective of whether your sack weights 2 kilos or 24 kilos the fact that you are running with this additional weight contained in a bag strapped to your back is bound to have some effect on your running ability and the more that you are aware of this then the more prepared you can be in your preparation and training.

21.1 The effect on your centre of gravity.

We all have a centre of gravity, that spot that is the middle where if we lean too far one way we fall forwards and if we lean too far the other we go backwards. This centre of gravity helps determine the way we move and our running style.

By putting a laden rucksack on your back this effectively increases the weight at the back of your body and moves your centre of gravity further back and this changes your running style and action. This has most effect on your angle of lean especially when going downhill and uphill.

When running downhill the angle of lean is the amount that you lean forward as you descend. The further that you lean forward, then the faster that you will run downhill. By having a heavier weight on the back, the angle that you can lean forward has to be reduced to prevent overbalancing and possible falls and stumbles and as a result descending speed will be reduced.

On uphill slopes as you run up, the angle of lean is the amount that you lean into the hill. The more that you lean into the hill then the more driving force is exerted by the muscles of the thighs and buttocks. Similarly as in descending, the angle that you can lean into the hill will need to be reduced to avoid overbalancing and falling forward, again this will reduce forward speed.

One other aspect that will make itself known is that with the extra weight and bulk on the back and the resulting change in the centre of gravity, then it can become more difficult to recover from a bad foot plant. The extra weight will encourage the ankle and foot to roll more to the side when placed on an uneven surface. This can lead to the runner becoming more cautious when travelling over rough terrain especially when trying to descend at speed.

21.2 The effect on your stride length.
Carrying a heavier weight does make it harder to maintain a longer stride length. You will find that your stride length will naturally shorten to keep as much of the increased bodyweight directly over the legs as possible. This will become most apparent when running downhill on shallower slopes where you would normally be accustomed to striding out and picking up a bit of speed.

21.3 The effect on your running speed.
As you would expect from carrying a heavier load your average running speed will fall. This is partially because:

1. The increased weight means that the muscles have to work harder to maintain the same effort.
2. The increased weight changes your running style so that your movement pattern is not at its most optimum.
3. The increased weight forces you to shorten your stride length.

In addition to these the extra weight increases your muscle's work rate thus speeding up lactate overload. High levels of lactate acid inhibit the muscles ability to perform and are one of the causes of exhaustion. This means that careful attention needs to be given to pace judgement. A slower running speed will need to be used in order to maintain acceptable levels of lactate within the muscles.

21.4 The effect on your energy consumption.
As you would expect from the points raised above, carrying an additional load will require additional energy consumption compared to running without one.

This being due to the extra work performed by your muscles and the need to power this work by energy consumption and this reflects itself in the feelings of hunger and exhaustion. Topping up energy stores by means of snacks/energy bars is a fundamental part of endurance running however be prepared to eat more often than you would normally expect than running without a rucksack.

21.5 The effect on your fluid consumption.

As with energy consumption above, because your bodyweight is effectively increased and the body is therefore working harder to carry this increased overall weight then as a result, it does generate more body heat during this process and will reach the over-heating stage faster than during normal running. This means that the runner will dehydrate faster than during an equivalent run without a load.

To compensate you will find that you will drink more often than you may possibly expect. Be aware of this and look out for the effects of dehydration.

21.6 Training while carrying full equipment.

The sole purpose of training is to condition both the body and mind to the demands required to complete your chosen event. As can be seen from the points raised above, running while carrying the load required for a mountain marathon places higher demands on the runner than on an equivalent run while unladen.

It is therefore essential to complete a proportion of your training runs under competitive conditions, i.e. whilst carrying full kit and this should be done on a regular basis. You should, ideally, complete between 50 to 75% of your long weekend runs with full kit. Any higher than 75% and you will start to lose your normal running motion.

A point sometimes made is using weight training to increase strength as an alternative to training with full kit. The body is a complex organism and as it moves there is a great deal of muscle and nerve co-ordination in order to provide this movement.

While weight training does increase your strength it does not necessarily train this specific muscle and nerve co-ordination. This can only be done by replicating the same movements that you are training for. In short, weight training can help but it can't replace training with full equipment over suitable terrain.

22. How Many Events Can You Do in a Year.

The answer to that would, to a large part, depend upon whether you would class yourself as a participant or a competitor.

For a participant the main thrill of the event is the taking part and competing against the course. They are not too unduly worried about winning prizes and, in fact, would probably be surprised if they did. The majority of competitors in any event are of this category. Because of this more relaxed attitude, there is no pressure to be at "peak physical fitness" for each event and so you will tend to find that these runners will, on balance, be capable of and will enter more events during the course of the year than the elite competitor.

On the other hand, a competitor who is expecting to be among the winning prize list will want to be in top condition for events. As a result they will tend to pick and choose the events that they enter. They will ensure that they have adequate recovery between marathons and that they are not over-competing. In short they will do fewer events during the year to make sure that they are in good condition for each of these.

However after saying that, with mountain marathon style events being held throughout the majority of the year, if you so wished it is possible to do an event nearly every month. So with that in mind what aspects need to be considered in making the decision of how often to compete:

1. Physical condition.
Even if you are not competing at the highest levels, the mountain marathon is a pretty gruelling event and your body can take a lot of knocks during the course of one. Injuries can and do happen, even such things as blisters can leave you in too poor a physical shape to contemplate your next one.

2. Recovery.
As a basic rule of thumb, it can take up to four weeks of recovery before you can effectively start to build up the training for the next marathon. On the plus side this build-up would not be from scratch as a high degree of conditioning would still remain from the training for the last race. Obviously this would depend upon the individual but on average you would be starting the new training phase at around 60% of the fitness that you started the last marathon at.

3. Training regime.
This flows on from the Recovery paragraph above. Using the recovery period and the higher level of fitness at the end of it, this could be used in one of two ways:
1. To either go into the next marathon at the same level of fitness by using a

reduced length training program or alternatively

2. Using the same length training program and then going into the next marathon at a higher level of fitness.

How you balance these out will be part of your annual training plan. However what this does mean is that there is a restriction on the number of marathons that you can enter each year if you want to maintain an effective training program.

4. Partner availability.
With it being a pairs event, two people need to make the decision to enter the marathon. If you have a regular marathon partner are they available for the same events as you, do they want to do the same events as you. If not then the situation arises of having to look for a suitable replacement partner and the question of do you actually want to run with somebody else.

5. Finances.
Entering a mountain marathon isn't cheap and the entry fee is just the beginning of the expense. Purchasing and/or renewing equipment and food plus the cost of travelling to and from the event all come into the equation. No matter how much we hate having to admit it, we all have a budget to live against and this may impose some restrictions on the number of events that we would like to enter.

6. Lifestyle.
We all have a particular lifestyle with various pressures placed on us by family, friends, work and from other sources. Participating in mountain marathons can actually be a relief to these pressures but it can also add to them. We all have to balance what we want to do and what we can reasonably expect to do without causing undue stress both to ourselves and to those around us and sometimes we just have to give a particular event that we want to enter a miss.

In short, how often and how many times you want to compete is down to the individual. There are enough mountain marathons out there to keep you happy which ever way that you choose and based on the constraints above you can make your own choice but remember that the most important thing about these marathons is to be safe and enjoy.

22.1 Suggested yearly training and event guide.
As mentioned above many people enter more than one marathon per year. Even if just doing this as a participant rather than a competitor, if you don't get the recovery period right in between marathons then you will be starting each subsequent marathon in a poorer condition than the previous one. By the end of

the year you could be physically less able than when you started the year.

As a general rule of thumb you should allow six to eight weeks between marathons for recovery and training. Any less and you open the possibility of the de-training effect described above.

As with all branches of athletics you have to accept that if you want your best performance then that can only happen in a limited number of events per year. Typically with a mountain marathon that will be in two events per year normally with three or four months between them. For example an event in June and then another in October.

However, one possibility that is available but is rarely considered is that of using the mountain marathon as a training event in itself. This can be done by entering a class that is lower than the one that you would normally compete in. By entering with a training perspective you would have the technical challenge of the navigation but without having the full physical challenge of your normal higher class.

With careful planning and self-control it is also possible to use early season events as "sharpeners" to test your ability and improve your fitness prior to your main event of the year. As you would be using these as training events, again, you need to compete in a lower level of class than you would normally enter. However, you can progress through the classes as you advance your training but then it becomes important not to compete too close to your main event. For example, possible training events leading up to the long score class in the OMM in October which would be the main event of the year:

1. April-Short score-Highlander
2. June-Medium score-LAMM
3. August– Short score-Phoenix
4. October-Long score-OMM

Don't forget that if you do take this approach then these events aren't your only training and they do need to be built in to a balanced training schedule.

PRE-EVENT PREPARATION .

Prior to setting off to the event there are a number of preparations that should be made so that at the start of the marathon both all of your equipment and you are ready for the off. Most of these are straight forward and involve nothing more than ticking a list but it is a wise person that does it.

Some controls are always going to be better approached from above. However, use common sense and when the control is at the foot of a crag then the best approach may be from above but coming in from the side.

23. In the Weeks Leading Up To The Event.

Straight forward preparation is simply making sure that you have the right kit, that it is in good condition and that it works. And this is all done in enough time to replace or repair if it is not up to the task.

23.1 Ensuring that you have all the correct kit.

A straight forward and logical step. All mountain marathons have a required kit list. Ensure that you have all of that kit and tick it off to the list. Do this at least the weekend before the event. Don't leave this to the last minute just in case you have to repair or replace some items. If you consider it helpful, make your own kit list. Start with the standard required kit list and then add to it your own personal and team requirements.

With these marathons being pairs events both partners normally contribute some items to the equipment "pool". Make sure that you both know which pieces you are contributing and that there are no misunderstandings and confusion.

In most cases, partners live fairly close to one another so it is worthwhile having a final meeting and running through the kit list together. This can also provide a good morale booster as a team.

However in some circumstances this may not be possible and the partners don't meet up until the arrival at the event. In this case it is even more important to make sure that you both know exactly which pieces of equipment you are both bringing and that you do actually bring it.

23.2 Ensuring that your tent is in good condition.

It is always useful to physically check over your gear at least a week before the event. This ensures that everything is in good order and that there are no nasty surprises waiting for the overnight camp.

Ensure that your tent has been fully dried out since it was last used. It is also advisable to erect and then re-pack your tent to ensure that there are no tears or rips in the fabric, that all the zips work and that all the guys, pegs and poles are within the pack. Its not pleasant getting to the overnight camp and finding a pole or peg bag missing.

Practice erecting the tent. You may have to put it up at the overnight camp in conditions of darkness and driving rain. Making sure that you can erect the tent both competently and quickly can make life a great deal easier.

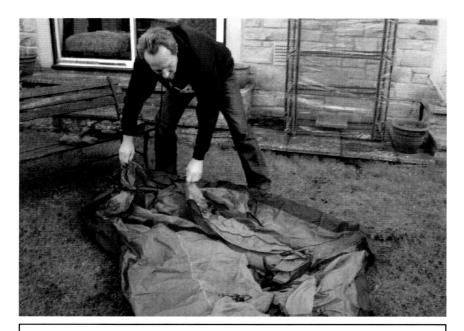

Practise putting your tent up. This will give you the opportunity to check it over and make sure that there are no tears or missing parts.

23.3 Ensuring that your cooking equipment is working and that you can use it.

The same applies to your cooking equipment as to your tent. Ensure all equipment is clean and dry and that the jets are clear. Set up and light your stove to ensure that it is working.

Use new fuel canisters/packs and make sure that you have enough for the weekend. If there are any special condition imposed by the organisers, such as having enough fuel at the end of the event to make a brew, then make sure that you have adequate supplies.

Tip. If you are flying to an event such as the Mourne in Ireland or one of the European races then be aware that you wouldn't be able to carry gas canisters in your luggage. You may need to pre-order them and pick them up at the event.

163

23.4 Ensuring that your torches and batteries are adequate and working correctly.

Always use new batteries. Check the torch housing for breaks or fractures and ensure that your torch is working properly.

Double check that your torch meets the requirements of the event's kit list and that you have got all of the required spares such as battery, bulb etc.

23.5 Deciding whether to stay overnight before the event or not.

At some point you will need to make the decision whether to stay overnight before the start of the mountain marathon or travel on the morning of the event. In many cases this decision will be made for you just by the sheer distance that the event is being held away from your home. Even though the exact location of the event may not be known until the final event details pack is received, the general event location, i.e. North West Highlands, Dartmoor, the Lakes, etc, will be known beforehand.

With most people, staying overnight before the event is a foregone conclusion irrespective of the distance involved as it makes the pre-start preparations so much more convenient. Registration can be done the night before so that there is no rushing around on the morning of the event, last minute preparations can be made and, basically, you can just chill out before the exertions of the following day.

Once that you have decided that you are going to stay overnight, you then have the choice of where you are going to bed down. This choice is down to personal taste and finances, most events have an overnight campsite for competitors to use or alternatively there are normally a range of bed and breakfast establishments, pubs and hotels within a relatively close distance to the event centre.

One point to note, when the final event details do come out naming the exact location of the venue and you have decided to book a B&B, hotel etc, then do your booking up fairly quickly. Rooms and beds get booked very early and if you don't get in quick then you may miss out and end up having to camp anyway.

23.6 Tapering down your training.

During your training program, as you get closer to the actual event, there should be an element of tapering, reducing your training level so that you are not tired at the start of the marathon. Stick to this tapering program and resist the urge to

Preparation and forethought is the key. All items of kit including the sleeping bag should be checked for damage and wear and tear and this should be done well in advance so that there is time to repair and/or replace.

do any extra training, it rarely works. You'll get more benefit arriving on the start line feeling refreshed and relaxed than you will from any last minute sessions.

23.7 Deciding of responsibilities

One aspect that often gets overlooked during the preparation process is the division of responsibilities, namely who does what on the day.

1. Who is the prime map reader.
At it's best, navigation should be a joint exercise but in reality no matter how good you are, one partner is going to be stronger than the other. This can have an effect on who does what as the better navigator can be preparing the route choice while the other partner can be doing other tasks.

2. Who carries the dibber and "clocks" in to the controls. One of the partners has to carry the dibber and dip it into the control box at the checkpoints. Generally

speaking this should be the navigationally weaker partner. While they are dibbing the dibber the stronger partner can then be making the route choice for the next leg.

3. Who is the better at compass work.
This may or may not be the better map reader. This comes to a fore when you have to run on a bearing in poor visibility, the partner who is the better at compass work would set the bearing while the other partner would act as the marker in the gloom.

4. Who is the stronger runner.
Ideally both partners should be of similar ability and fitness however things don't always work out that way in real life and one partner may be fitter than the other. In this case always remember that this is a team event and that you get no prizes for just one partner finishing the marathon. Always let the weaker runner set the pace, having them constantly trying to keep up with the faster runner can spoil the enjoyment of the event putting pressure on the partnership and can lead to premature exhaustion for the slower runner.

Despite good intentions there is always going to be the probability that one partner is going to be slightly fitter than the other on the weekend of the event. This may cause bad feeling and frayed tempers when one partner has to constantly wait for the other to catch up. Regular training together as a team before the event can identify problem areas like this and get the pair working together.

24. In the Days/Hours Leading Up To The Event.

This is the last minute preparation of gathering and packing your gear, preparing yourself, travelling and getting to the event and making sure that you are all ready to stand on the start line.

24.1 Final event details.

After entry, the final event details are sent to you just prior to the event. When these are sent out and the method by which they are sent out differs from event to event, for example the OMM send the details out by post two weeks before the event while the LAMM sends the details by email just two days beforehand. However during the entry process for your chosen marathon, it will tell you when and how to expect your final details.

Depending on event, the final detail pack may be sent out to each individual team member or to just the nominated team contact on the entry form.

When you receive your final details the pack will normally contain:
1. The required kit list.
2. Location of the event centre.
3. The opening times of the event registration.
4. An indemnity form which you need to sign and hand in to registration at the event.
5. Your team number.
6. Your team start time.
7. If the event does T-shirts and you have bought one, confirmation of purchase.

From this pack you are required to take with you to the event and hand into registration the following:
1. A ticked off kit list confirming that you have all of the required kit.
2. The signed indemnity form.
3. Your team number.

Failure to hand in any of these will probably lead to a refusal to your team starting the event.

It would also be advisable to take with you the confirmation of any T-shirt purchase.

167

24.2 Taking on fluid and energy.

In the last few days before the marathon you should be ensuring that both energy and fluid levels are topped up as much as possible. This is not a licence to eat anything that you like, but rather, the opportunity to consume as much of the correct carbohydrate and starchy food as possible. This should be accompanied by a steady fluid intake over the same period. Drink small volumes but often.

Carbohydrate and fluid should go hand in hand. The body can't store carbohydrates, which provides energy, without adequate fluid reserves while at the same time fluid can't be stored without the carbohydrate.

Keep drinking small and often all the way up to the start line and if you feel the need to take in an energy bar while travelling on the event bus or waiting for your start then do so.

24.3 Tapering down your training.

Over the last couple of days before the event you should be following your pre-planned tapering down routine. Basically this should involve doing virtually nothing. Any training done now will not have any beneficial effect on your performance in the marathon, it is far too late for that. What it will do however is tire you and deplete your energy stores .... just what you need before a big event !

Instead training should be focussed on allowing your muscles to relax and stay loose. Training runs should be no more than one or two miles and run at a very slow and comfortable pace, in fact the slower the better.

The day before the event no training should be done. The reality is that with the packing, the travelling to the event and registration then you probably wouldn't have time anyway. However, with the travelling the likelihood is that you will arrive slightly cramped from being cooped up in the car and so at some point after you arrive a good walk should be taken to help stretch out the muscles and prevent stiffness. This can also be followed up by some gentle stretching exercises.

24.4 Kit preparation.

By this stage of the game all the major items of kit such as tent, cooking equipment etc should have been purchased or otherwise obtained, it should have been inspected for damage and to ensure that it is working ok. You should also be familiar with and capable of using it all even in bad weather.

Pack your competition rucksack well in advance. Make sure that the heavier, bulkier items such as the sleeping bag go towards the bottom of the sack. If done correctly, once packed you should not need to go back into this sack again until the event commences.

You should also have all your food and energy drinks purchased and ready to go. All of this will be dehydrated or pre-packed in one form or another and it is not as if you are going to be carrying fresh food, so why wait till the last moment to get it ready.

Keep an eye on the weather forecast to see whether you may need to make any last minute additions or deletions to your kit such as taking a heavier-weight fleece or adding sun cream.

Do a last minute kit check against both the event required kit list and also your own team's list of what each partner is carrying. Then pack your rucksack. Now try it on, see if there are any areas that are digging into your back or causing potential rubbing and chafing, if necessary adjust the load so that it is comfortable on your back.

All this should be done so that your event rucksack is fully packed and sitting by the front door long before you set off for the event. You should now not need to go into the sack itself until the event has started. And if you are leaving your packed rucksack next to the front door, then don't forget to put your fell shoes next to it.

If camping overnight before the race make sure that you have all your base camp kit and food ready, packed and in the car. The last thing that you want to do is to have to start using your event kit or food just because you weren't as thorough with the base camp check list as you were with the event one.

24.3 Travelling to the event.

Travelling to the event itself can sometimes be quite stressful which is not what you want just before a weekend's intense activity. Try and take as much of that stress away by:

1. Making sure that you have a suitable route planned from your home to the event HQ and include planned rest breaks at suitable intervals. The longer the journey the more important the rest breaks become in order to avoid arriving tired and irritable.

2. Check whether there are any travel disruptions expected on your planned route such as road works, etc. Use the websites of the Highways Agency, the AA and the RAC, you may have to change the route of your journey to avoid any particular black spots.

3. Expect to experience delays on your trip, the longer your journey then the more chance that this will become a reality. Think about having an alternative route to the event centre just in case you do end up being diverted away from the one planned.

4. Leave plenty of time for your journey. This is especially important if actually travelling on the morning of the event but this also needs to be borne in mind if travelling the day before. Much better to arrive early and have to kill time than arriving too late for the registration and not being able to start the event.

5. If you are travelling to the event by plane then take your competition rucksack and kit into the cabin with you. Don't put it into the hold as luggage, just in case it goes missing. However, with current security arrangements note that all energy drinks, gels, etc will need to go into your bag in the hold or they will be confiscated at check-in.

6. Also if flying and using car hire at the other end, make sure that you have your car reservation details and other documentation with you. Easy to forget while you try to remember everything needed for the race.

7. In these financially austere times with the price of petrol increasing every week and global warming continuing apace, it is possible that we could be doing

Before you leave for the event do a quick check to make sure that you haven't left anything on the kitchen floor or tucked away anywhere else.

more to reduce the number of car journeys that are made to events. Look at car sharing or using transport laid on by organizers to from key points.

24.4 Registration.

The event registration is normally open on most events from 1600 hours on the day before the start. The exact times will be given in the final event details. The registration opens the day before to allow those competitors who travel early the chance to register and to avoid congestion at the registration during the morning of the event.

During the registration process you will be asked for:
1. A ticked off kit list confirming that you have all of the required kit.
2. The signed indemnity form.
3. Your team number.

Failure to hand in any of these will probably result in refusing your team to start the event, so make sure that you take it all with you to the registration. The final event details will tell you exactly what you need to take to the registration. Depending on the event, you may be asked to produce your team kit and this will be inspected. Some events perform an actual physical check of your equipment to confirm that it is all present while others will accept a ticked off list that has been signed and confirmed by the competitors. Physical kit checks may not be performed on every competitor, these may be done as spot checks by choosing teams at random.

At the registration you will be signed in to the event and confirmed as participating. If for any reason you do not start the event or pull out at any point during the weekend then you **MUST** inform the organisers. Failure to do so could result in the emergency services being called out to search when you fail to turn up at the finish and also having you being barred from all future events.

The registration hall.

At the registration you will be given:

1. The map of the course, although with some events this may be given out at the start of the first day.

2. Your electronic dibber (see The Event section for more details on the dibber).

3. If the event is using bus or an alternative transport to travel to the start then you will be given some form of boarding pass.

4. Any last minute changes to the final event details that have previously been sent to you.

5. Any last minute changes to the competition area such as out of bounds areas, however, as an alternative these may also be given at the start.

Normally at the registration the team will be given a copy of the event map although practices do differ from marathon to marathon and with some events it may be given at the start. Some may give two maps, one per partner, while others may just give one with the option to purchase a second copy. The map itself may be waterproof or non-waterproof and you may be given some form of plastic map bag. Alternatively you may be given a non-waterproof map but with the option of buying a waterproof copy. All options have been used by various marathons in the past.

Go through the registration process as soon as possible after arriving at the event centre. There are normally longer queues on the morning of the event and leaving your registration to the last minute always runs the risk of delay with the result that you miss your start time.

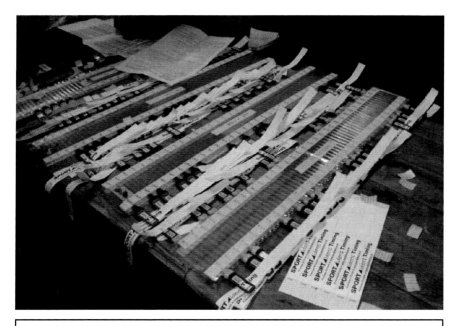

Dibbers waiting to be collected at registration.

24.5 Staying overnight.

On the assumption that you are staying overnight, on arriving at the event centre you have a number of options depending upon your choice of overnight accommodation. If you are planning on staying at a B&B, pub, hotel or other form of premises then you should have made your booking soon after you had received confirmation of the venue in order to ensure that you had a bed. The alternatives would be camping in the event field or even possibly sleeping in the car.

Whichever choice you make, the priority when you arrive at the event centre should be to register your entry. After that you can relax and take it easy with no pressure until the next day.

If you have chosen to spend the night in some form of accommodation then there will be no need to break into your competition kit. Your rucksack can stay unopened and ready packed either in your room or the boot of your car.

If you are camping then resist the urge to use your competition gear for the overnight camp, leave the tent, cooker and other paraphernalia safely tucked up in your sack. Take a complete second set of kit, tent, cooker etc, to use as a base camp. This doesn't have to be lightweight gear as the carrying will be done by your car, so go as heavy and as comfortable as you want, anything you like so that your overnight is as easy and relaxed as possible.

The logic behind the two sets of kit is to keep your lightweight competition kit as clean, dry and tidy as possible. Use it for the pre-event camp and if it rains or is damp then you could be trying to put a wet and heavier tent back in your rucksack on the morning of the event and this will also apply to other items of your kit. Much better to keep this dry and well-packed ready for the start line.

Tip. If possible try and bring a pair of wellies for use at the event centre and the pre-event camp site. In wet weather they can be a lot more comfortable than wet trainers.

24.6 Preparation checklist.

Below is a short preparation checklist to help you pull everything in Sections 23 and 24 together. It's simple but effective, so use it.

174

Task	Completed	Comments.
Correct kit list as per event.		
Tent erected, all pieces in place and checked for wear and tear.		
Cooking equipment working in good order.		
Fuel ordered		
Food and drink for whole event purchased.		
Shoes cleaned and check for any wear and tear.		
All paper work completed.		
Route to start prepared.		
Friday night accommodation arranged.		
Navigation equipment working		
Rehearsal of rucksack packing.		

THE EVENT

Once you have been booked-in through registration you are then ready and waiting for the start of the event. For those that are new to mountain marathons then participating can be a little unnerving. In this section of the book we look at the various procedures that are applied at the start and what happens during the event itself.

The start never gets delayed for rain !
The occurrence of "inclement" weather is one of the challenges of this type of event. At times you may be togged up in your waterproofs right from the start.

---

25. The Start.

For the uninitiated the actual start of a mountain marathon on Day 1 can be a confusing and puzzling affair and at times this confusion can also apply to seasoned competitors. The section below lays out the procedures that are normally followed at the start of a marathon and will take you from the point of standing outside the registration centre to beginning running on the course.

However, you need to bear in mind that these events are always very much individual events, which is part of their charm, and procedures may differ slightly from event to event and also from year to year. At the registration you will be given instructions for the start and so you should read and absorb these.

25.1 Where do you report to.
At the registration you will be given your instructions for the start of Day 1 and these will include your start time and the location of the starting point. The location will generally be in the form of a grid reference and can be close to the registration centre or a bit of a distance away from it. There is a growing practice with some events to have the start quite a considerable distance away from the event centre and that does require a bus, train or boat trip to the start which is all organised as part of the event arrangements. Irrespective of whether you walk from the event centre or from the disembarkation point of a bus, the route to the actual starting area is usually very well marked and on arrival you'll notice a mass of teams each waiting for their call to the starting grid.

25.2 Who do you report to.
At the starting area there will be a number of marshals milling around doing various tasks and you would report your presence to the marshal who is organising your class at the beginning of the starting grid or alternatively if you have not done this at the registration, the marshal who is clearing off the dibbers (making sure that any existing data on the dibber is deleted).

25.3 The layout of the starting grids.
The starts of all mountain marathons utilise an orienteering-type grid system comprised of a number of boxes made out of marker tape. Normally each class would have its own row and within that row would be a number of boxes normally either two or three. An example of a grid is shown below which is broken down into what is called a two minute call.

178

A Start	B Start	C Start
1 minute to next grid	1 minute to next grid	1 minute to next grid
1 minute to next grid	1 minute to next grid	1 minute to next grid

The purpose of the grid is to control the movement of the participants and to ensure a strict time control over their release onto the course.

Lining up on the starting grid.

25.4 Moving through the starting grids.

While you are gathering at the start keep your ears open as one of the marshals will be announcing start times. When your start time is called enter the first of the boxes that are there for your class. Normally only one team will be entering each box at a time. A loud noise, such as some form of klaxon, will be sounding at one minute intervals and as it sounds you will be directed to move up into the next box along the row. When you are stood in the last box and the klaxon goes then your event will start and you will be released by the marshal to start running.

Make sure that you arrive at the start with plenty of time in hand to meet your call-off time. If you turn up late then you may be allowed to start as and when

179

you can, in this circumstance there may be more than one team in a particular box.

Also ensure, if you have not already done so, that your dibber has been cleared.

25.5 Event maps.

As mentioned in the section on registration, you may be given your event maps either at registration or if the maps are pre-marked, then at the start. If the maps are being given out to you at the start then this will normally be while you are standing in the last box or alternatively you would pick them up just as you exit it.

Also at this point the control descriptions for each class may be given out either attached to the map or pre-printed on the map itself.

Alternatively if the event is using master maps for you to mark-up the controls and out-of-bounds areas onto your own event map then there will normally be an area just in front of you where these will be displayed. Make your way over to them and, making sure that you are at the correct map for the correct class, mark-up your map. Make sure that you accurately record **ALL** the controls that you need to visit on to your map.. You will then be able to start the course.

If marking up the map, take the time to do it correctly and both of you check that it is right. Taking care here can save you a lot of time later when you are looking for a control that has been marked in the wrong location on the map.

26. Day 1.

After you have left the starting grids take some time to make your route choice to the first checkpoint. At this stage your route choice can be quite basic to the point where you are just heading in the right general direction. This can be refined as you travel and get into your stride. Remember to take care locating the first checkpoint as this can set you up for the remainder of the day. A bad first checkpoint can snowball giving you a negative mental attitude that can be carried on through the other controls resulting in a very poor day. On the other hand, a good first checkpoint can mentally put a spring in your step making you positive about your navigation for the rest of the event.

When you see the kite of the first checkpoint, approach it but remember to check its individual control code against the checkpoint description list before you dib your dibber. Sometimes controls are placed fairly close together and it can be quite easy to go to the wrong one.

While one partner is dibbing the dibber the other can be starting to determine the route to the next checkpoint. After dibbing move away from the checkpoint as quickly as you can, your presence there makes it easier to spot the control and

Following a line to the control.

you may be handing an advantage to your opposition.

Leave the first checkpoint to move to the second and make your way round the course from control to control.

As you progress through the day remember your plan on re-hydrating and replenishing your energy stock, eating and drinking in other words. Also monitor the weather conditions as you go, this may affect your route choice and your clothing.

26.1 The finish of Day 1.

As you progress round the course you will come to the penultimate checkpoint and from here you will navigate to the final checkpoint of the day, which will be fairly close to the overnight campsite. In most cases the campsite itself will be visible during the final stages as the course will tend to descend from higher ground down towards it.

At this final checkpoint there are usually a number of marshals and two or three dibbing boxes. Unless there are different overnight camps for different classes, all the competitors will pass through this final control which may cause a little congestion. Dib your dibber in one of the boxes to record passing through the

Day 1 finish.

final checkpoint and the marshal will then direct you to a tent or a similar area where you will be presented with a paper read-out giving timings and checkpoints visited during the day. The dibber itself is retained for use on the second day and is not handed in to the marshals or checkpoint staff.

This is one of the beauties of modern electronic timing, a virtually instant record of the checkpoints that you have passed through and when. Take the time to check your paper read-out carefully, if there are any discrepancies or if you think that something is wrong or incorrect then now is the time to report it to the checkpoint staff. If your print-out is all correct you can leave the finishing area and move off into the overnight campsite.

27. Overnight.

The joys of the campsite and spending a night under canvas. The overnight camp on a mountain marathon can be enjoyable, passable or just unpleasant and a lot of that you can make for yourself. The following are a few tips to help you get by.

Overnight camp.

27.1 Selecting a camp spot.

The first step after passing through the finishing procedures is to get to the camping field and get your tent up. The tent will provide cover if the weather is inclement and it will also give you somewhere to just "flop" out.

Depending upon your finishing position on Day 1 then your options of where to pitch your tent may be limited. If you want the choice of an empty field then you better finish first !!

However, where you place your tent can have a considerable effect on how much you enjoy your overnight stay:

1. Try and avoid any stony ground. This will make placing your tent pegs far easier and will also give you a softer surface to lie on, karrimats do have their limitations.

2. Obviously try and avoid any sloping ground, nice and flat should be the order of the day although it doesn't always work out that way and you may have limited options.

3. Try and position yourself close to a field wall. The wall will help protect you from prevailing winds and other elements. It will also limit the directions from which people can walk past your tent, other competitors passing your tent during the night could disturb your sleep.

4. Try not to get too close to any water course. Midge's are a curse at the majority of the overnight camps and putting a bit of distance between you and their source may help reduce the numbers that will eventually find their way to your tent.

5. Not too close to the source of the camp's drinking water. It's always nice to

Priority after getting the tent up and changing out of any damp clothing is to replenish energy and fluid. Get a brew on and start preparing you meal.

feel that you don't have far to go to collect your water but everybody else has to go there as well. This may mean that you may find yourself on the main thoroughfare to the drinking water complete with all the disruption that can cause especially late at night when you are trying to sleep. You need to come up with a balance of not too far but not too close and not on a line that is going to become the obvious way to and from the water supply.

6. Not too close to the toilets. This is the same situation as with the drinking water but with the increased probability of disturbance during the "wee" hours of the night as people make their way to and from the loo.

7. Lastly, not too close to the neighbouring tents. If it rains during the night, tents that have been pitched to close have been known to become waterlogged.

27.2 Preparing a meal.
The next priority after setting the tent up is getting the evening meal on the go in order to replace the energy used during the day. While you are waiting you can always be snacking on any titbits that you have left over from the day's running food. More details on the evening meal and other food is provided in the Food and Drink section.

27.3 Rehydration.
As with the food, now that you have finished running you need to get as much fluid into your system as you can to ward off the effects of dehydration and prepare for the next day. Remember - drink little and often.

27.4 Results Day 1.
At some point during the evening the Day 1 results will be pinned up on the notice board. Unless you are one of these people who stay with the nose pressed against the board until they appear, then the first that you will hear about them will be the rumour going round the campsite that "the results are up". As usual there will be a rush to see them but if you want to avoid the crowd you can always pop along later as they will be there all night. Make a point of seeing them as you may be surprised and find yourself in the chasing start for Day 2 and will need to know your start time. For an explanation of the chasing start system see the section on Day 2.

27.5 Sleep.

Sleep, the essential. Without this you wouldn't perform that well the following day, so how do you ensure that you get a good nights sleep ?

First off, there is no way that you are going to sleep as well as you do at home no matter how tired you are. So during the week before the marathon try and ensure you get your rest. Put sleeping hours into the bank, reduce the late hours, try and avoid any pressure and keep things relaxed. It will pay in the long run.

At the overnight camp avoid partying all evening with your pals and get an early night. Late to bed wouldn't do you any favours and certainly wouldn't win you any friends with the rest of the competitors. Add a pair of earplugs to your personal kit, these will help keep unwanted noise away, some of which may be coming from your partner's snores. Keep warm, it is difficult to sleep when you are cold. If necessary put on an extra couple of layers.

Remember to set your watch for a wake-up call and allow plenty of time for breakfast, toilets, taking down the tent and travelling to the start.

27.6 Breakfast.

Get the stove going as soon as you wake up and get a hot drink and food into you. The sooner that you have breakfast the less chance there is of it lying heavy on your stomach when you start to run. Remember to keep drinking.

See the Food and Drink section for the contents of breakfast.

27.7 Toilets.

Being a mountain marathon the competition area itself is in wild, mountainous terrain although the overnight camp is generally in a slightly more civilised location both for logistical and environmental reasons. Several hundred competitors at an overnight camp can have quite a significant environmental impact on a relatively small area.

Nowadays most mountain marathons have the familiar sight of the tall blue boxes, otherwise known as portaloos, at the overnight site although in the past the practice of a plank above a slit trench was not unknown. Obviously the provision of portaloos has made the whole experience of toilet visits a much more pleasant occasion and has drastically reduced the environmental impact of these events. One noticeable exception to this is the LAMM where on some years there is still the option of using the portaloo or the traditional slit trench.

In a practical sense, somebody somewhere must be calculating a ratio of portaloos per competitor and in the overall scheme this must work, however, whenever YOU want to pay a visit then you can guarantee that there will be a long queue. Obviously the busy times for the toilet queue are going to be before everybody turns in for the night and the next morning after breakfast till just before the start. If somehow you could organise your body clock to avoid these times then it would be more convenient but, in reality, you are going to end up queuing.

And despite the queues please be patient and don't "go" behind a wall or similar places. At a recent LAMM, instructions were contained in the final event details not to do "al fresco craps" away from the toilet area. This can cause problems for the organisers with the landowners.

Be prepared, with the number of competitors on these events and with most of them eating dehydrated food, by the morning of the second day these portaloos can start to be a bit smelly. Also as part of your personal kit, always carry an amount of toilet paper to take with you to the loo. That is the second guarantee after the queuing, the portaloo will always run out of paper just before you get into it.

The early morning visit ....

27.8 Breaking camp.

Ensure that you break camp and get it all packed away in your rucksack with plenty of time to spare so that you can get to the start line with time in hand. If it is raining it will take you longer to pack up your tent and gear and so make allowances for that.

Prepare your running kit for the day ahead. Fill your water bottles and put all your running snacks in the various places so that they are readily at hand during the day.

Leave no rubbish. Feel free to discard any gear that you no longer need and that the rules allow you to get rid off including such things as empty gas cartridges. But everything that you leave, place in the appropriate waste disposal site and do not leave on the camping field. However, if in any doubt where to leave it then take it back with you in your rucksack - after all you brought it in !

28. Day 2

28.1 The start.

The start of Day 2 is different to that of Day 1 with a chasing start being used for the leading competitors of each class and then a mass start for all the other participants.

A chasing start is where the leading team is set of first and then the following teams are set off at intervals corresponding to the time that they are behind the leading team after Day 1. For example the leading team will set off at, say, 07:00; if the second team are 10 minutes behind them after the finish of Day 1 then they will set off at 07:10. If the third placed team are 15 minutes behind the leading team after Day 1 then they will set off at 07:15 and so on.

The leading runners that set off under the chasing start may be decided by the positions after Day 1 such as the top ten teams or they may be decided by time such as all teams that finished within an hour of the leading team's time. This will be dependent upon event. In the LAMM the leading teams are judged by position and the top ten teams in each class are given a race number to wear on Day 2, in most other events this is not done and numbers are not issued.

All other competitors will be set off together in a mass start normally one hour after the leading team has started. In the example we are using this would be at 08:00.

The board posted at the overnight camp that gives the results and finishing positions of Day 1 will also provide the start times for Day 2. This will tell you whether you are one of the leading teams going off in the chasing start and give your start time or one of the teams going off in the mass start and what time that goes off at.

Provisional details of the Day 2 start times such as what time the leading team sets off and the time of the mass start will be included with the event details that are sent to you prior to the event.

Normally the competition area remains the same for Day 2 as it was for Day 1 and so the same map is normally retained but in some cases where the map is pre-marked, a new map may be given with the Day 2 checkpoints marked on it. Where a new map is not given, a new control description list will be available at the start of Day 2 listing the checkpoints to be visited that day. The new map/control description list will be available at the start either just before or just after the start line. So as you make your way to the start line pick one of these up and make sure that you have picked up the correct class. You wouldn't be the first to make that mistake.

The dibber that you have retained from Day 1 needs the data from Day 1 cleared off making it free for Day 2. A dibbing box to do this is available either just before or just after the start.

Whether you are in the chasing start or the mass start make sure that you arrive at the start line with plenty of time to spare. Once you have been released by the starter Day 2 begins.

Tip. If using the same map for Day 2 as for Day 1 then think about crossing off the Day 1 controls so that there is no confusion with those used for Day 2.

28.2 The day.

On Day 2 the same basic procedures and rules apply as on Day 1. Ensure that you take care locating the first checkpoint of the day. Getting this right has just as much relevance as it did the previous day in getting you into the correct frame of mind. It is too easy to be complacent after Day 1 and to then make an elementary error.

Progress your way round the course until you come to the last control from which, depending upon event, you may follow a flagged or taped route back to the finished area.

28.3 The Finish.

The finish procedure on Day 2 is fairly similar to that at the end of Day 1. When you enter the finish area the first requirement is to dib your dibber in one of the finishing boxes to signify that you have completed the course. You will then be funnelled by the marshals to receive your time printout for your Day 2 run.

As with Day 1 it is important to quickly check this as you only have a limited opportunity to query it. The line of finished competitors will then be moved along to a point where a marshal will remove the dibber wrist strap from you. Once removed you will then exit the finish area.

At this point there will be a place to discuss any issues with your Day 2 timings. Other than this your event is now completed and you are free to go home, have the after race meal, collapse in a heap or …...what ever else you have planned.

AFTER THE EVENT.

A mountain marathon doesn't end when you pass through the finish and hand in your dibber. There are still the not quite so simple matters as eating and drinking, travelling home, recovery and preparing for the next marathon. In this section we will look at these aspects of the event.

In the higher standard classes such as the Elite, Klets or A class, controls may be situated on what is called sites of "elevated interest" where you may encounter a little bit of exposure to a steep drop.

29. Travelling Home.

By their nature mountain marathons are held in the back of beyond which means that the majority of competitors do have a reasonably long journey to get back home again from the race venue. Despite the adrenaline coursing through your veins from a, hopefully, successful completion you will still be fatigued and physically drained from the exertions needed over the weekend. So the importance is, to get back home safely.

The first step is to try and replenish both food and fluid stocks and this is also part of your recovery as shown in the next chapter. Most marathons do some form of post-race meal, however, this is not normally sufficient to sustain you on your trip home unless you live relatively close to the event.

Have something tucked away in your car to both eat and drink and make sure that you have enough. Start eating and drinking as soon as you get back to the car and tuck into them regularly on the way home. This food and drink is part of your recovery program so make sure that it is compatible with what you have

Heading home with the event souvenir.

planned. However, remember that you have just spent the weekend on dehydrated food and energy bars, your post-race food will seem a lot more attractive if it is something different !

With the excitement of just finishing the event you may not be fully aware of how fatigued you are. Make sure that you take plenty of rest breaks on the way home. These give a good opportunity to take on board some additional food and drink and just as importantly the chance to stretch those rapidly aching muscles. So take a small walk and don't just sit around in McDonalds.

If you feel the need have a quick forty winks before you set off from the event centre. Sometimes a quick snooze can do a power of good.

The important thing is to use common sense and to get home safe.

30. Recovery.

As with all athletic events a period of recovery needs to be taken after completing the race before embarking on the next phase of the training cycle. However because of the nature of the mountain marathon the recovery period is longer than most other events. Unfortunately this catches many runners out and they allow insufficient recovery before they return to full training and this can start a spiralling de-training effect.

The recovery period can be split into three time zones:

1. Immediate - which is the time immediately after the event and in the hours following.

2. Short term - which is the first and second days after the event.

3. Long term - which is the period after the second day leading up to four weeks after the event and with some individuals may even last as long as six weeks.

30.1 Immediate recovery
During these immediate hours after the event the priority will be on nutrition. Basically feeding fluids and calories into the body in order to restore salt levels, vitamins etc. Be aware of the "magic" period for the first 15 to 20 minutes after exercise stops when the body is more responsive to absorbing fluids and topping up energy stores and try to consume both as soon as possible. Also a recovery will be helped by a period of damage limitation, in the hours immediately after the marathon the muscles will start to stiffen up especially on a long drive home. Keep them loose by regular movement such as little strolls and stretching.

Be prepared for your stomach to react a little unfavourably to your diet over the two days of the marathon and also to the level of exertion achieved. This doesn't happen to everybody but if you are unlucky then it could last a couple of days. You may also get the same results if you have consumed some "bad" water over the two days.

30.2 Short term
The short term is the two days after the marathon and during this period the emphasis moves from nutrition to damage repair. Initially on the first day you will still be consuming fairly high volumes of food and drink, your body will be telling you to do this through hunger and thirst so don't ignore it. As the first

day passes into the second reduce the amount of your intake down to normal levels, especially food as you don't want your weight to start increasing. However, if you are still feeling the need for fluids keep drinking. On the first day the muscles in your legs, back and shoulders will probably start aching and this will become worse on the second day. This is where the damage repair comes in and the intention is to keep the muscles as relaxed and supple as possible.

During the course of the marathon you may have taken a knock or two, or twisted an ankle. In which case, if they are suitable for you, then you may wish to take some over the counter anti-inflammatory medication such as Ibuprofen. Gentle exercise such as walking should be performed to stop the muscles stiffening up and this can be coupled with some gentle stretching. The current fad among elite athletes are ice cold baths to repair muscle damage, but this is down to personal taste and you may prefer regular hot baths to keep the muscles relaxed and allow the hot water to stimulate the blood flow through the muscles which in turn helps the healing process. Mentally the exhilaration of finishing the marathon will have worn off and you will be feeling tired and lethargic. Relax, over the next few days this feeling will wear off especially after a couple of nights sleep.

30.3 Long term.

The target behind long term recovery is to get you back to running at your normal training levels as soon as possible. Unfortunately many people underestimate the amount of recovery that is needed after an event such as this and return to normal training too soon. Full training while the body is still tired actually has a detraining effect, Instead of improving your physical condition as planned, you actually deteriorate with your running ability reducing in an ever decreasing circle.

During the first week after the marathon you should be looking at doing virtually no running with just a small amount of recovery running towards the end of the week. Usually no earlier than the Friday. Recovery running is very slow, easy running at your slowest possible speed and only for a distance of two or three miles. During this week your mileage will be far less than 10% of your normal weekly mileage pre-marathon.

In the second week mileage will be upped to 25% of your normal weekly mileage. However running pace should still be kept way down at an easy, relaxed level. Again keep the distance of your runs down and keep the regularity of the runs down as well so that you are having a rest day in between each run.

In the third week mileage can be upped to around 50% of your normal weekly mileage. Running speed should still be kept down to the easy, relaxed pace of previous weeks. The distance of the runs should be no more than 5/6 miles although the regularity can be increased so that you only have two rest days this week.

During the fourth week mileage can be increased to around 75% of your normal weekly mileage. Running speed should still be kept down to an easy, relaxed pace although a couple of the runs can include an element of faster paced running but not at too high a pace. The distance of the runs can now be increased but kept below 10 miles. Take one rest day this week.

In week five, you should now be back to normal training mileage although speed work should still be refrained from for the next two weeks and then gradually reintroduced.

Remember that this recovery program is suggested and not compulsory. While we wouldn't recommend taking a shorter recovery period and running a higher mileage than that shown here, do listen to your body and if you feel the need to take longer to return to full training then do so.

31. Preparing for the Next Event.

On the assumption that you have enjoyed your experience of the mountain marathon and that you have arrived home safely and are in the process of recovery from your exertions then now is the time to reflect.

It is decision time .... do you want to do another mountain marathon ??

If you do, then now is the time to review your performance.

The most important question is, how did the teamwork go ? Did you and your partner get on, did the pair of you gel, was there friction and crucially is it now the time to look for a new partner ?

You then need to review the class that you entered. Was it too much of a challenge or was it not enough of a challenge, do you want to move up or down a class or were you happy with the one that you have just completed ?

Next you need to look at your own performance both as an individual and as a team. This needs to be done from two angles from both the physical fitness side and also from the aspect of skills. Where did your fitness let you down, was your training program effective, did you stick to it, could you improve on it and if so what elements could be improved ? Did you have problems with the navigation, was it just simple basic errors or was it something more complex, did you feel comfortable navigating, do you need to look at improving these skills by perhaps going on a navigation course ?

Finally you need to review your kit. Was it adequate, what worked and what did not, if you are now going to get into these marathons do you want to splash the cash and get some lightweight gear ? Now could be the time to start preparing a "wants" list.

And now you enter your next mountain marathon. Depending upon both your physical shape and also the lateness of the year, you may have time to enter another event or, alternatively, it may be better to wait till next year. Either way you now need to get back on to the training ladder and start the whole adventure again.

HEATH AND SAFETY.

With all things modern, health and safety rules. In this section we have put together a few notes on various miscellaneous matters that may affect your health, safety and just general comfort while on an event. Hopefully you'll never need to worry about any of these although it is a safe bet that you wouldn't avoid the midges.

Most of the notes here will be familiar to the experienced mountain marathoner, however, for those new to or not quite so experienced with these marathons then it may be advantageous to read. The incident on the LAMM 2010 where two competitors fell a considerable distance and suffered significant injuries does prove the need to be prepared.

With up to a thousand competitors taking part in some mountain marathons, certain parts of the courses may develop "little trails" due to the sheer number of runners passing through. When these are encountered try to follow them rather than creating new pathways. This keeps environmental damage to a minimum and helps ensure that the ground cover returns to normal as soon as possible.

32. Medical.

This book is not meant to be a medical journal and we have made no attempt to go into any detail on medical matters. Instead we just offer some general advice on what to do if you are competing and you have a known medical condition and also if you start to feel unwell during the course of the marathon.

32.1 Known medical conditions.

Many medical conditions do allow you to take part in physical activities and, depending upon the condition, there is no reason why competing in a mountain marathon can't be one of them, however both you and your doctor know your condition in more detail and if you have any concerns always consult your doctor before entering the event.

1. On the entry form, be it electronic or paper, there should always be a space for you to notify the organisers of any known medical condition that you have. Always be open and honest here and don't contemplate concealing anything, having this information may be very useful to anybody providing you with assistance if an "incident" does happen.

2. Make sure that your partner is aware of any medical condition that you have and, if you feel it necessary, how they should react if anything happens. It can be quite a shock if, for example, your partner suddenly has an asthma attack or epileptic shock when you didn't even know that they suffered from that condition.

3. Make a point of carrying your medication, if any is used. Work on the assumption that the worst will happen and that you will need it.

4. Carry a card or something similar that states what your medical condition is and what to do if anything happens. Make sure that your partner is aware that you have the card and where it is, just in case it is needed and you are not in a position to hand it over.

32.2 Feeling unwell during the marathon.

If you start to feel unwell during the course of the event then the first thing that you must do is to stop and take an assessment of the situation. Without taking the "I'm a brave solder I'll make it to the end no matter what" attitude make a reasonable assessment of whether you can or should carry on. Even if you decide to withdraw then there may still be an element of carrying on in order to get to a checkpoint, roadside or other point to withdraw or gain assistance albeit you will probably be travelling at a reduced pace.

In the worst possible scenario where you don't feel that you could carry on or that continuing even to a place where you can get assistance would make the situation worse, then you have no choice but to summon help.

32.3 Hay fever and other allergies.

Expect the worst and always take your medication with you. If you don't need it then you have only carried a few extra grams. If you do need it then it can make the difference between a successful competitive weekend or two days of miserable, feeling lousy underperformance.

33. Injuries.

Injuries can, and will happen. The first action is to do a realistic four point assessment and by realistic what is meant is a calm structured thought process with none of the gung-ho "I've started so I'll finish no matter what the cost" attitude which normally ends up making the whole situation worse.

Perform an assessment:

1. Is the casualty capable of finishing the course albeit at a much reduced pace.

2. If the casualty can't finish the course can they then make it back to the event centre under their own steam following the straightest and easiest route.

3. If the casualty can't make it back to the event centre then can they, either with or without assistance, make it to the nearest road or track where rescue would be easier.

4. If the casualty can't be moved then make them comfortable and summon assistance.

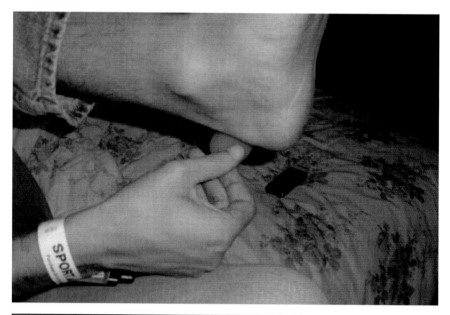

Appling second-skin to help prevent blisters. If using these or tape to protect your feet, always make sure that you carry enough spare for Day 2.

In many cases it will be fairly straight forward under which category the casualty lies but always err on the side of caution. In the event of head or back injuries always keep the casualty still and summon assistance.

With minor injuries and dependant upon your own abilities the injury may be treatable with your own first aid kit.

33.1 Blisters, bruised feet and damaged toenails.

In many cases running over rough country for two days while wearing minimal footwear can cause blisters, bruised feet and damaged toenails. The scale of these injuries may be minor compared to other possibilities but these can have a big impact both on your comfort and performance over the two days.

Experience has taught many of the competitors that prevention is better than cure and so a significant number of runners either tape their feet or use commercial products such as Compeed or similar.

The theory behind both the tape and the "second skin" is to place a protective layer between the foot and the shoe to protect from rubbing and chafing.

34. Hypothermia.

Hypothermia is a condition where the body temperature falls to such an extent that it can become, potentially, life threatening.

When competing in mountainous environments such as with a mountain marathon then the effects of weather fluctuations can have a severe effect not only on performance but also on personal safety. Hypothermia is caused by an imbalance between the body's production of heat and it's heat loss which results in the body losing more heat than it produces. In the mountains the body's heat loss can increase quite rapidly in a short space of time due to any or all of the following:
1. Adverse weather conditions
2. Poor clothing for the relevant conditions.
3. Over exertion.
4. Poor physical condition.
5. Low food intake
6. Possible medical history and/or other problems.

There are three classes of hypothermia. The normal body temperature is 37 degrees centigrade. When this temperature falls to between 35-34 degrees then this is classed as mild hypothermia. A fall to 33-32 degrees is moderate hypothermia and a fall below 32 degrees is classed as severe hypothermia. The obvious necessity is to recognise the onset of hypothermia and take corrective action long before it reaches the severe stage.

The onus of recognising the symptoms will normally fall on the affected person's partner as one of the indicators is the inability to recognise your own body temperature. Victims of severe hypothermia have even been known to remove their clothing believing themselves to be too warm.

Indicators to keep your eyes open for include
1. General slowing down of movement.
2. Shivering.
3. Minor behavioural irregularities.
4. The extremities such as the hands and legs are cold.

As this develops into moderate hypothermia look for
5. Marked slowing down of movement and thought.
6. Increased shivering although in advanced cases this may stop.
7. A confused state of mind.

8. A cold skin.
9. The skin developing a white or waxy colour.
10. The heart rate being lower than expected.
11. Respiration will drop and become shallower.

If caught soon enough the situation can be rectified by just putting your jacket on to conserve body heat but if the situation is worse then treatment will consist of:

Preventing further heat loss
1. Stop all further activity.
2. Stop heat loss by insulating the victim from the ground.
3. Stop heat loss by providing shelter.
4. Stop heat loss by increasing the surrounding air temperature.

Promoting external re-warming
5. Wrap the casualty in spare clothing, sleeping bags, survival bags etc.
6. Shelter the casualty in a tent.
7. Place at least one other person in the sleeping bag with the casualty in order to raise the temperature within the bag.
8. If conscious give warm but not hot drinks and also high energy food.

In general, the male sex is more susceptible to hypothermia than females. This is due to the additional third layer of subcutaneous fat on the female body that helps provide additional insulation.

If you get to the position that you have to take the above steps then that is the point where you need to summon help and seek medical assistance.

35. The Effects of Heat.

Cold and wet weather are not the only environmental conditions that can affect the mountain marathoner. Excessive heat can also give problems if not given due consideration.

As described previously, the body's normal temperature is 37 degrees centigrade and this is maintained by various mechanisms such as:
1. Sweating.
2. Alternating the size of the peripheral blood vessels.
3. A decision to remove or add clothing.
4. Controlling the environmental temperature.

35.1 Heat exposure.
Excessive heat affects the body in a variety of ways. When exercising in a hot environment, heat builds up inside the body and the body automatically reacts to get rid of this heat through the sweating mechanism. If the body loses large amounts of water and salt from sweating then the sweat control mechanism of the body malfunctions and shuts down resulting in heat stroke (sometimes called sunstroke).

35.2 Heat cramps.
Heat cramps are muscular pains and spasms resulting from the loss of water and salt from the body. Excessive sweating may result in painful cramps of the muscles of the abdomen, legs and arms. Heat cramps may also result from drinking iced water or other cold drinks either too quickly or in too large a quantity after exercise. Heat cramps are usually an early sign of approaching heat exhaustion and indicators include.
1. Muscle pain and cramps.
2. Faintness or dizziness.
3. Nausea and vomiting.
4. Exhaustion and fatigue.

If you suspect heat cramps do the following:
1. Move the casualty to a cooler area.
2. If the casualty can drink give half a glassful of cool water every 15 minutes but stop if the casualty vomits.
3. Gently stretch or massage the muscle to relieve the spasm.

4. Request medical assistance if the casualty does not respond.

35.3 Heat exhaustion.
Heat exhaustion is caused by the excessive loss of water and salt through sweating. It is the most common condition from exposure to hot environments.

Heat exhaustion is caused by:
1. Heat or an in tolerance to heat.
2. Inadequate fluid intake.
3. Failure to recognise the early symptoms and take rest.

Signs and symptoms of heat exhaustion include:
1. Pale, cool moist skin (clammy).
2. Large dilated pupils.
3. Normal or below normal temperature.
4. Rapid and shallow breathing.
5. Headache, nausea, loss of appetite.
6. Dizziness, weakness or fainting.

Treatment of heat exhaustion is aimed at cooling the casualty.
1. Stop the casualty doing any further activity.
2. Move the casualty to a cool and sheltered place.
3. Reduce the casualty's temperature by sponging and improving the air circulation.
4. If the casualty is conscious and can drink then give half a glassful of cool water every 15 minutes but stop if the casualty vomits. Do not give salt tablets.
5. Remove the casualty's clothing but do not allow them to become chilled.
6. Request medical assistance.

35.4 Heat stroke.
Heat stroke, also known as sun stroke, is a life-threatening emergency. It is less common than heat exhaustion and despite it's name it is not necessary to be exposed to the sun for it to develop. Here the casualty experiences a breakdown of the sweating mechanism and is unable to eliminate excessive body heat. If the body temperature rises too high then the brain, kidneys and liver may be permanently damaged.

Signs and symptoms of heat stroke include:
1. A temperature of 41 degrees centigrade or higher.
2. Hot, wet or dry and reddish skin.
3. Small constricted pupils.
4. Headache, nausea, dizziness or weakness.
5. Deep and rapid breathing at first, then shallow and almost absent.
6. Fast and weak pulse.

Treatment for heat stroke includes:
1. Stop the casualty from doing any further activity.
2. Move the casualty to a cool and sheltered place.
3. Monitor the casualty's breathing and circulation.
4. Reduce the casualty's temperature by sponging and improving the air circulation.
5. If the casualty is conscious and can drink then give half a glassful of cool water every 15 minutes but stop if the casualty vomits. Do not give salt tablets.
6. Remove the casualty's clothing but do not allow them to become chilled.
7. Request immediate medical assistance.

36. Exhaustion.

Exhaustion can and will hit each member of the team during the course of this two day event. The mountain marathon is very demanding on the body and over the two days you can virtually guarantee that at some point you will have a bad moment. The extent, length and effects of this period of exhaustion will, to a large part, depend upon how quickly you can spot what is happening and how you react to it.

In most cases it is not the competitor who is suffering that is first to spot the signs but rather the non-affected partner. However, sometimes as a result of the exhaustion, the affected partner may refuse to admit the situation.

Do not be afraid to admit to tiredness and slow down or even stop to rest, in the longer term this will be more beneficial to overall team performance than just soldiering on. If caught at the early stages, exhaustion should not give too serious a delay to your team timings. However it is crucial that the non-affected partner is supportive during this period and helps to get the team back on track.

Spotting it.
1. Trips and stumbles can indicate a deterioration in physical coordination due to tiredness.

2. Brain coordination also deteriorates resulting in poor decision making, obvious navigational mistakes are a good sign of the early symptoms of fatigue.

3. The affected partner will become increasingly uncommunicative and any response to questions will tend to be very monosyllabic.

4. Other possible physical signs would include abnormal sweating or shivering.

5. The affected partner would be continually wanting to rest and lag behind.

How to stop it.
1. Exhaustion mainly comes from a lack of available energy so take regular stops and eat high energy snacks.

2. When it hits don't be afraid to slow the pace down or even stop, top up your energy stores by eating and just as importantly rehydrate.

3. In extreme cases get shelter, eat and drink. Do not simply "continue on". If necessary find an escape route.

If in any doubt seek medical assistance.

37. Ticks.

Ticks seem to be becoming more of an issue in certain parts of the country. They live in dense undergrowth and as animals, such as deer and sheep, pass through they jump and attach themselves to the body where they then proceed to feed on the animal's blood. To a tick, as you pass through the undergrowth looking for checkpoints, you are just as good a source of a meal as any animal and so there is always the potential to pick up a few of them on the exposed skin.

Although unpleasant there is not normally any problems with tick bites provided that the tick is removed correctly. However, in certain parts of the country ticks are known to carry Lyme Disease which does have the potential to be serious and, in rare cases, can be fatal.

Removing ticks from your body can be difficult as the front end of the tick, the head, burrows into your skin to feed on your blood. It is important to get the whole body out including the head as leaving this in can cause infection.

Some of the more traditional methods of removal are no longer accepted practice, for example:
1. Do not leave the tick in until they drop off.
2. Do not attempt to pull out with tweezers as the probability is that you will leave the head inside.
3. Do not cover the tick with petroleum jelly or alcohol as in some cases this can make the tick sick and cause it to vomit into the blood stream.
4. Do not use the hot head of a burnt match or cigarette end as it rarely removes the head.

As an alternative special tick removal tools can be obtained from most vets or pet shops. Although designed for animals they are usually just as effective on humans.

Seek medical help if at all worried about the effects of Lyme Disease.

For more information on ticks and Lyme Disease have a look at the Borreliosis and Associated Diseases Awareness UK website at www.bada-uk.org

38. Midges.

The midge, a mean nasty biting little fly that is only an 1/8th of an inch long but, despite its lack of size, it is one that can make your life hell. This fly is not really encountered during the day while running but is a very regular companion at the overnight camp and quite often in large numbers. It can be a real pest.

There are over thirty species of midge native to Britain however only five of these that actually target humans. Which is quite lucky really!

Midges thrive wherever there is moist vegetation such as bogs and wet moorland. The wet, acidic soil provides the perfect environment for breeding and enables the pupa and larva to remain moist, if they dry out then they die. The midges just love a calm, damp, overcast day even with some light rain, or areas of shade along the edges of woods and forests where they can find protection from sunlight and the wind.

The thing that may surprise you is that midges are vegetarians. The male stays vegetarian, quietly sucking nectar and sap from plants for all of his life. However, it is the female midge that when pregnant gets the craving for blood. Prior to being fertilised by the male she is just as happy sucking sap as he is but once mated she needs a meal of blood within two to five days in order to ensure a healthy start to life for the young. Isn't it nice to know that when you get bitten you are ensuring the survival of the species ....

One other aspect of a midge bite is that when a female finds a nice meal i.e. you, she then gives off a chemical called a pheromone which acts as an attractant to other females. This stimulates the mass attacks by hundreds or even thousands of midges during the height of the season.

Midges are most active during early morning and late evening however they can and will bite at any time of the day. The trigger that seems to set them off is the level of light. If the light level falls below 260 watts/m2 then the female is stimulated into seeking a victim. Which explains why they don't like bright sunny days.

The midge season stretches from the beginning of May till around the end of September with June, July and August being the worst months. The lower temperatures of late autumn and early winter kill the little fella's off.

So what's the best way of avoiding them:
1. Wear an insect repellent that works for you. Some makes and types work better on some individuals than others.
2. Wear lighter colours, midges, like most insects, seem much more attracted to darker colours especially black.

3. Cover your arms and legs when they are active. Consider a midge net for your head.
4. Try and avoid areas where midges gather. Try and pick a spot where there is direct sunlight and a slight breeze. Midges can't stand bright light and are forced to seek shelter in winds of excess of 3 mph.

If you are allergic then think about carrying some form of antihistamine cream or tablets. These may help sooth the area and keep inflammation and irritation at bay. Seek medical help if required.

39. Calling for Help.

Hopefully you will never need to do this but in the event of a serious injury to either you or your team-mate how do you summon help.

With the mountain marathon being within a relatively confined area and the probability of a fairly high number of competitors within this area then you shouldn't be too far from other people who will assist you to summon help. The first step is to use your whistle to attract the attention of your fellow competitors and inform them that you are in need of assistance. The international distress signal using a whistle is to blow three sharp blasts and then wait a minute before repeating the three blasts.

If you are in the dark then the use of the whistle is replaced by the use of the torch. In this case, flash the torch three times, wait a minute and then repeat.

Some mountain marathons don't allow mobile phones on the event but even so considering the locations in which these events are held then the probability of getting any signal is quite low. As a result this normally means finding the nearest telephone or manned checkpoint to seek help.

Erect your tent and put the casualty in a sleeping bag within the tent while somebody, preferably from another team, goes for help. If possible it is always advisable for the team to stay together as you would be familiar with the casualty and would be more likely to keep them relaxed and at their ease, you may also have information about the injured person that may be useful to the rescue services when they arrive.

Ideally someone should stay with the casualty at all times, although if you cannot summon assistance from fellow competitors then you may have to leave your team-mate on their own while you seek outside help. The priority here is to get help even if it means leaving the casualty alone for a period.

Make a note of the location grid reference, any nearby features, the time, the nature of the casualty's injuries and if they have any known underlying medical problems. Check the map for the nearest telephone, which may be in a telephone box or a dwelling such as a farmhouse, or alternatively the nearest marshalled checkpoint. Obviously go for the nearest be it phone or checkpoint as speed is of the essence.

However be aware that not all checkpoints are manned and in most cases you cannot tell from the event map whether they are or not. Nor do all checkpoints, even if manned, have contact with the outside world, only a proportion of checkpoints on any event may have radio communications. The leading event in this aspect is the OMM which generally has manned checkpoints and manned checkpoints with radios identified individually on the event map.

If you go for the phone then telephone the 24 hour emergency phone number that is shown on your Control Description Sheet and ask for a suitable message to be passed to the mountain rescue team including the telephone number that you are calling from. Stay by the phone as the rescue team may phone back for further details and information. Don't leave the location of the phone until the rescue team have confirmed that it is ok for you to do so.

With some events the procedures for summoning help will be included within the event literature forwarded to you prior to the event. Always worthwhile making a note of these in case there is something arranged that is specific to that event.

40. Giving Assistance.

Mountain marathons are held in wild, remote countryside and that is one of their attractions. Unfortunately it is also one of their downsides, when anything goes wrong help is not sitting readily at hand. This means that the competitors in a mountain marathon have to be self-reliant to a very large degree and it also means that if anybody does get into trouble, then it is expected of you to help them to the best of your ability.

Mountain marathoners are self-reliant but they also know when to band together to help each other out and it is expected that a marathoner will abandon their own race in order to help a fellow competitor who is hurt or injured. The overriding principle is "I don't know when I may need help and so I should be prepared to help others when they need it".

If you hear the three blasts on the whistle head towards the source of the noise and be prepared to give whatever assistance that is necessary. This may involve going for help, waiting with the casualty or even "donating" some kit or clothing to help keep the casualty warm.

However, after saying all this, whenever you go to help someone whether it is your own partner or another competitor, then first do a safety assessment. Don't ever put yourself in danger or at risk by helping an injured person. This sounds selfish but turning one casualty into two does not improve the situation in any way and you would be much better summoning more professional help such as the mountain rescue.

41. Waiting for Help.

While you are waiting for help to arrive, what do you do ?

Firstly, stay where you are, your rescuers will be looking for you at your last known position (LKP) which will have been forwarded to them. If you are not there then they will have to start searching for you. Only move position if it becomes dangerous to stay where you are through such things as changes in weather or unstable ground conditions.

Make your position as visible as possible to help guide your rescuers in towards you. This may be as simple as fixing a bright piece of clothing to a tent pole so that you can wave it.

Stay together. Once the initial party that has gone to summon help has left, then the remaining members of the group should stay together to provide help and support to both the casualty and each other.

Stay positive and calm. Reassure the casualty and keep morale high especially if it takes longer for rescue to arrive than you expected.

Keep everybody warm. It is vital that the casualty is kept warm but also other people who are helping and who will be dressed in lightweight kit. They will very quickly become cold now that they have stopped running and the last thing that you want to do is increase the number of casualties. Add layers of clothing and if necessary erect tents as shelter. Have warm drinks and food although don't provide these to the casualty unless they are conscious and you are certain that they have no internal injuries.

Last but not least, monitor the condition of the casualty. You don't need to note actual measurements, unless you are actually in reality a health care professional and know what you are doing. Rather it is a case of observing the casualty's condition and being aware of whether it is improving, deteriorating or stable.

42. When Help Comes.

To put it simply, do what you are told. When the mountain rescue arrive they will take charge of the situation and will follow their own laid down procedures and protocols. You will generally be asked for information on the incident and what happened and, if the casualty is not able to answer for themselves, for any possible background information such as personal details and any known medical history of the casualty.

Follow the instructions given by the mountain rescue which in many cases will be to stand to one side and relax. Occasionally you may be asked to assist in some format but, again, if asked to do anything you will be given full instructions by the mountain rescue personnel.

43. Withdrawing from the Event.

When you first arrive at the event centre you will register for the marathon and be recorded as a participant and given your dibber. From that point on, your progress round the course will be recorded.

If for some reason you do decide not to start the race, then you must report back to the organisers at the event centre to officially withdraw. The same procedure also applies if you withdraw while actually out on the course or if you fail to start Day 2.

News of your decision to withdraw must be passed to an official of the event and to the event centre. Quite often checkpoints are not manned or even if they are may not have a method of communicating with the event centre. So even though you may have told somebody of your withdrawal you still have to physically report in to the centre to notify them and hand in your dibber.

Failure to do so could result in you still being recorded as being out on the course and when you don't show at the finish this could result in a full-scale search being mounted by the emergency services. If this happens then it will also result in you being disqualified from all future events.

Always retire from the event via the event centre.

44. Erosion and Other Green Issues.

Organisers work hard on planning the routes and keeping the environmental impact of the event to a minimum. One of the considerations that they have to bear in mind is not to overlap the courses too much in order to keep land use and possible erosion problems to a minimum. Despite this, it is inevitable that "crocodiles" or long lines of runners will happen at certain points of the courses especially towards the end of Days 1 and 2 when everybody is moving towards a common finishing point. Whenever these occur, try and keep to the path made by the passing of the runners in front and try not to widen it or create a new one by doubling up alongside another pair of competitors. The land and vegetation will regenerate quicker if this erosion is kept to a minimum.

As a final note remember the phrase "pack in, pack out" and take all your waste and rubbish with you. And this means from both the overnight campsite and your "during the day" snacks. Leave no litter to spoil the landscape and that includes banana skins, not a natural or pleasant sight to see in the mountains.

45. Appendices

45.1 Governing bodies.

The following organisations are the governing bodies of the sport of fell, hill and mountain running within the UK.

The Fell Runners Association	www.fellrunner.org.uk
N. Ireland Mountain Running Association	www.nimra.org.uk
Scottish Hill Runners	www.shr.org.com
Welsh Fell Runners Association	www.wfra.org.uk

ACKNOWLEDGEMENTS

Although the two author's names appear on the cover of this book there are many more who helped in it's preparation from allowing the use of their photos to reading draft copies of the book, acting as models and making suggestions as to what to include. All of this has been gratefully accepted and incorporated into the book and so in alphabetical order we'd like to give thanks to the following, experienced mountain marathoners one and all.

Patrick Bonnett
Daniel Brison
Alan Hunt
Steve Gustard
Steve Lumb
Harry Manuel

About the Authors

Both the authors have been active outdoor people for many years and learnt their navigation skills at an early age. As solo fell runners Stu and Kev have both competed in the full spectrum of events ranging from long distance fell and mountain running, to orienteering, to mountain marathons. But both have always had a soft spot for the challenge presented by the Mountain Marathon and over the years have competed in many events around the country.

Being qualified fell and hill running coaches, both men have, over the years, instructed and taught the fine art of navigation to fellow club members and other interested runners and have also run a popular series of low-key mountain marathon courses for club members and others.

As a runner, Stu has been and still is an active competitor, even on occasion winning some races but recently he has turned his focus to devising and then going on to run new long distance rounds. These new routes include the Durham Dales Reservoir Round, the Durham Hewitt's Round and the North Pennine YHA Round. On the mountain marathon circuit his record includes:
Open Country MM 2002, 4th overall, 1st Vet team.
Lowe Alpine MM 2004, Elite course 9th overall, 1st Vet team.
Lowe Alpine MM 2005, Elite course, 12th overall, 1st Vet team.

Although a proficient navigator and very enthusiastic competitor, due to a basic inability to run as fast as other people, Kev has never managed to achieve the same level of competitive success as Stu. But that never stopped him trying.

The Run Off-Road Series

Run Off-Road is the name adopted by Trailguides for it's publications aimed at the fell, hill, trail and mountain runner. This series of books is designed to promote the sport of off-road running in all it's many forms and to encourage the participants to improve and develop their abilities and skills in order to further increase their enjoyment of the sport.

This is an evolving series of books that is constantly expanding. See our website at www.trailguides.co.uk and subscribe to our newsletter for regular updates on our range of publications.

At the time of writing the titles in the series include:

An Introduction to Trail and Fell Running
Downhill Techniques for Off-Road Runners
Uphill Techniques for Off-road Runners
Terrain Training for Off-road Runners
Mountain Marathon Preparation
Navigation for Off-Road Runners
Long and Ultra Distance Off-Road Running
The Mountain Marathon Book

Coming soon
The Trail Running Book

Disclaimer

The information contained in these pages is provided in good faith, but no warranty is made for its accuracy. The contents are, at the time of writing and to the best of our knowledge, up-to-date and correct. However, the world is a changing environment and what is correct one day may not be so the next. The suggested training regimes contained in this publication are exactly that, suggested. It is the reader's responsibility to judge their own level of fitness and whether they are capable of performing any of the said activities.

No guarantee whatsoever is provided by the authors and their team and no liability is accepted for any loss, damage or injury of any kind resulting from the use of these pages. Nor as a result of any defect or inaccuracy in them.

As with all outdoor activities, you and you alone are responsible for your safety and well being.
